I0459572

Leading With Grace

Cultivating Hope, Authenticity, and a Focus on People Throughout the Leadership Lifespan

JULIA BIALESKI

DEDICATION

For the teachers and mentors who have modeled graceful leadership on my journey.

And - for my family, without whom I could not teach, lead, or write.

Table of Contents

Introduction

Principals are the heart and soul of schools. We need principals and other committed school leaders to educate and support children for generations to come. I was most certainly aware of this need during my time in the role, but the idea for this book was born in the months that followed my transition from principal to district-level leadership. I realized that I had stories to tell that would have helped me when I started my journey as a principal. In reflecting on my experience, I noticed common themes that I was able to apply to my work throughout a variety of situations. I found myself writing to process the emotions that accompanied an end to such a significant portion of my professional and personal life. In reflecting on my tenure as a principal, I realized that there were many lessons from that time that I wish I'd learned earlier in my career. I am intensely committed to contributing to the sustainability of our profession. If you are a principal, assistant principal, coach, dean, or aspiring school leader, this book is for you. If you are new to your role, new to your school, or if you are feeling stuck and questioning whether you are in the right place, this book is for you.

Writing a book has been a lifelong dream of mine. As a child, I was drawn to fiction. I spent hours upon hours writing stories on an electric typewriter in my bedroom. I filled pages with stories, which I bound in construction paper covers, and envisioned a future as a professional writer. At that age, I never would have imagined that this would be the book I'd one day write. Despite the fact that I have not (yet) produced the great American novel, being a lifelong writer and lover of books has nevertheless served me well in the development of this book. This book has been a passion project, and it is in many ways my love letter to the career that brought me professional and personal fulfillment, pushed me to be a better human being, and gave me the gift of making a difference in the lives of children.

I am a learner at my core. I loved school as a child. From a young age, I was drawn to working with children, and in hindsight, have always been destined to be an educational leader. In third grade, I wrote and directed a play, which my teacher allowed our class to perform for our parents and the other classes in our school. At twelve years old, I began running summer camps for neighborhood kids and friends of my siblings out of my parents' backyard. I babysat on every available weekend during my teen years, and volunteered in my mother's nursery school classroom during college, before declaring elementary education as my major, and subsequently devoting my career to children as an educator.

Over the past twenty years, I have been an elementary school teacher, served as an instructional team leader, written curriculum, planned and facilitated professional learning at the school and district level, and led three vastly different elementary schools as an assistant principal and principal, before most recently making the transition to district-level leadership.

While I have undeniably been a leader for decades, it was not until I transitioned into the role of principal that I truly felt comfortable labeling myself with the title of leader. It was not the title of principal that gave me the confidence to step into the label, however. It was the fact that as a principal, I finally found the opportunity to lead in a way that was completely and totally authentic to who I am as a person.

The challenges that I faced and lessons that I learned as a principal not only shaped my professional career, they altered my life. Serving as a principal allowed my confidence to grow, brought me a new perspective on the level of influence I had on others, and produced a tremendous amount of joy. My time as a principal also brought about many unexpected challenges, for which I was not prepared during graduate coursework or while sitting in leadership development sessions. Despite these difficulties, I found success in the role by remaining true to myself, focusing on people first, and making decisions grounded in my core values.

Serving as principal was, undeniably, the best job I have ever had. I loved the job, and I know I will never love a job the same way again. In my five years in the role, I experienced countless joys: greeting hundreds of children at the door each day by name, hearing the delighted snickering of second graders who'd won the right to duct tape me to the wall by exceeding a monthly reading goal, dashing through the hallways during a rainy, indoor Halloween parade dressed as Cruella DeVil while screaming, "Where are the puppies?" to giggles and gasps from students, and getting pied in the face (twice, by the same first grader!) at my very last evening event before leaving my school. In what other profession would these memories be among your highlights?

I served as an elementary school principal in a large, high-performing suburban district in Maryland for nearly five years. Our school served 640 students in preschool through fifth grade, and housed a regional Academic Life Skills program for students with intensive disabilities working on an alternative curriculum framework. As principal, I directly supervised 115 staff members, supported a large, diverse community of parents and families, and collaborated with leaders from the other 77 schools in the district to consistently implement policies and procedures. For those five years, I rarely went to the grocery store, stood in the TSA line at the airport, or attended a sporting event for my own children without running into students and families. I needed to be "on" all the time, both inside and outside of work. I often felt like the mayor of a small town.

When I accepted the position in 2019, I was aware that I was taking on a challenging and important role, but had absolutely no way to know just how challenging the next several years would be personally and professionally. As a principal, I navigated the COVID-19 pandemic, the politicization of schools, tragedies in my school community, and the myriad day-to-day challenges of the work of school-based leadership. Through my experiences, I have reflected on the leadership actions, strategies, and mindset that led to my success during extremely challenging times.

As a first-year principal, I had a strong and supportive cohort of principal colleagues in my district, encouraging district level supervisors, and a talented leadership development team providing me with ongoing coaching and professional learning. I certainly would never have made it beyond my first year without their support. Of course, I also read books, articles, newsletters, and blogs to help me be the best I could be in the role.

Leading one of 78 schools in our large district meant that I was also constantly comparing myself to my colleagues, many of whom had me beat when it came to years of experience on the job. Serving in such a large district required a keen sense of the political context that came with the job. Despite the many fantastic supports around me, when the job was its most challenging, I struggled to find a resource that both provided me with actionable, practical strategies that I could immediately put into practice while also hitting all of the right notes for me to continue to feel hopeful and remain resilient. During the hardest moments, I felt unsure of myself, questioned my competence and my ability to do the job, and sometimes wanted to give up.

The work of educators, particularly those of us in leadership roles, gets more and more difficult every year. Educators are leaving the profession in droves each year, and fewer and fewer young people are choosing education as a career path as they enter college. The pipeline is narrow, and it's no different for administrators. Many teacher leaders see the challenges and obstacles that their principals face on a daily basis, and they choose not to pursue higher level leadership as a result. Even the superintendency is impacted, with about half of the 500 largest districts in the United States seeing superintendent turnover between March 2020 and September 2022, according to Education Week.

My hope for this book is that it will serve as an invaluable, timely resource for other educational leaders. Even though I share my experiences through the lens of a principal, this book will be beneficial for school leaders in many different roles, because the lessons are universal to leadership. Regardless of our school levels, the sizes of our districts, our geographic locations, or the professional development resources and supports available to us, we share a common bond as leaders. This book is for each and every educational leader committed to making a positive impact on the lives of children and communities. If you sometimes question whether you have what it takes to lead, I am here to tell you what I needed someone to tell me when I stepped into the job: You **can** do it, and you can do it with grace.

What is Graceful Leadership?

"A leader takes people where they want to go. A great leader takes people where they don't necessarily want to go, but ought to be."

-Rosalynn Carter

Be Brave, And Care About People

On the day our staff returned to work for the new school year, we gathered in the cafeteria for breakfast. Fresh-faced and ready for the year, 115 staff members greeted one other, sat together in teams enjoying coffee and food, and chatted about their summers. The energy in the room was high, but I couldn't deny that people were also eager to get to their classrooms and begin tackling their long to-do lists to get set up for students the following week. Each summer as a principal, I walked this tightrope between capitalizing on the time we could spend together as a full staff and honoring the need of my teachers to have personal time to work uninterrupted in their classrooms. Both were important. Finding that balance was always difficult, and this year was no different in that respect. However, this was August 2021, and it was the first year we were fully reopening in person following the pandemic. We had not gathered as a full group like this since my first year as principal in 2019, having spent the previous August reopening virtually. This first gathering carried a heavier weight than it would have during a typical year.

That morning, I knew that there were mixed emotions in the room. As I stood at the front of the cafeteria, observing as everyone ate breakfast, I saw laughter and smiles from some teachers. Sitting next to those smiling teachers were others who were teary and visibly uncomfortable. Many of us were excited to return to a sense of normalcy after two years that were decidedly not normal. At the same time, people felt disconnected from one another, and some felt disconnected from their work. The return to a work routine following a summer break is challenging. For a group who had spent the past year and a half adjusting all of their trusted routines, stress levels were already high, and the children hadn't even returned yet. As the principal, I was simultaneously feeling excited, relieved, and nervous. I was aware of the impact that my words and actions would have on our staff to kick off the week. I could not miss the opportunity to use my position to set a course for my staff for not only that day, but for the entire school year.

When it was time to turn on the microphone, I kicked us off with an exercise called the *Six Word Story*. According to legend, Ernest Hemingway once won a bet by telling a story in six words: "For sale, baby shoes. Never worn." I challenged our staff to summarize their purpose for serving as educators by telling their own six word stories.

After a few seconds of silence, a few smiles broke through. People started talking and writing. Like any good teacher, I gave ample wait time, and when it seemed everyone had jotted some thoughts down, I encouraged our staff to share their stories with one another. As everyone moved throughout the room, I again noticed mixed emotions, but the overall mood in the room had shifted. People were still smiling and laughing, and there were still a few tears. However, this time, the tears were paired with smiles as emotional teachers read their six word stories to one another. The energy was different. I could sense hope, enthusiasm, and connection among colleagues. When it was time to share, a few members of the staff volunteered to read their six word stories to the entire group. One teacher started with, "This was a little heavy for the first day back, but I'm glad we did it. I needed it." Teachers, support staff, front office secretaries, and members of the custodial team read their six word stories with pride.

I encouraged everyone to take their six word stories and keep them prominently displayed somewhere in their classrooms, where they would see them each day that year. We all need an opportunity to be reminded why we do what we do, and my hope was that by placing our six word stories in a visible place, they would serve as inspiration and motivation on challenging days.

Before I sent the staff off to work in their classrooms for the remainder of the day, I projected one final slide on the screen. It was my six word story, and to me, it summarizes graceful leadership in only six words: **Be brave, and care about people**.

The Case For Graceful Leadership

The role of the modern-day school principal is complex and nuanced, and the job can feel overwhelming and lonely. Principals are the center of their communities, serving as the face of their schools. The scope of the job, time demands, and accountability pressures continue to increase each year. The role gets more and more difficult every year, and no matter how many additional tasks we add to our plates, nothing ever seems to come off in return. Running a school day after day can be exhausting, and it is easy to get caught up in the seemingly never-ending sense of urgency that comes with the role. In education, we are in the business of people, serving students, families, and the community. Our work is deeply personal, and we must arrive prepared each day to face any situation that could arise. This is important, impactful, meaningful work. It is also often thankless and isolating.

In order to effectively lead staff, support students, and engage families, school leaders must show up at their personal best each and every day. Graceful leadership is a mindset that can help us to build endurance, foster hope and resilience, and connect with those around us in order to maintain the stamina necessary to do this important work. Leading with grace is not a solution. It is a way of showing up both inside and outside of work. This mindset of graceful leadership can help ensure the longevity and sustainability of our profession as school leaders. According to the National Center for Education Statistics, 11% of principals left the profession between the 2020-21 and 2021-22 school years across the United States. This approach is critical more now than ever.

Graceful leadership does not only benefit principals. Principals cannot lead their school communities alone. Teacher turnover rates follow a similar trend as school and district leaders, with teachers also leaving the profession in droves. According to the National Center for Education Statistics, teacher turnover rate increased by 5% from 2013-2023. Schools in the United States were estimated to enter the 2023-2024 school year with a shortage of 100,000 teachers, with urban areas and low-performing schools disproportionately impacted by the nationwide teacher shortage. The National Education Association (NEA) found in a 2022 poll that 55% of surveyed educators reported planning to leave the profession earlier than anticipated, citing burnout as the number one cause of this early departure. A high degree of teacher turnover has a direct, negative impact on students both academically and social-emotionally.

Research has long told us that effective teachers are the most significant factor in determining students' academic achievement. According to rand.org, teachers have two to three times more impact on reading and math performance than any other factor, including leadership. Students develop strong connections and relationships with their teachers, and strong student-teacher relationships improve attendance, self-regulation skills, and motivation for students. Graceful leadership can help to reduce burnout for teachers and nurture longevity in the profession for the educators we support.

It would be an oversimplification to suggest that one leader be able to single handedly reverse the national teacher shortage. However, we should not underestimate the influence of a great leader on a school community. With graceful leadership, we can provide necessary support to teachers and staff to encourage them to remain in their jobs. A positive school climate, intentional actions to improve working conditions in a school, and opportunities for professional growth and development can all be addressed through graceful leadership. Suggestions for how to address these through graceful leadership will be explored in more detail in Chapter 5.

In other words, graceful leadership in a school can, for some teachers and staff, be the difference between leaving the profession and making the commitment to stay.

Defining Graceful Leadership

Graceful leaders act authentically to themselves, while prioritizing genuine, strong relationships with all stakeholders. They model vulnerability with others, while projecting confidence and authority. They engage in clear and frequent communication, while leading with empathy and respect. Graceful leaders remain focused on supporting students, families, staff, and their larger school communities while never losing sight of the need to prioritize their own wellbeing. Graceful leaders are brave, and at the same time, they care about people.

In many ways, graceful leadership requires us to walk a delicate balance between seemingly conflicting attributes. Adaptability is a key component of graceful leadership. Graceful leaders must be prepared to respond to any situation, and must feel comfortable adjusting their leadership style to the needs of the situation. Therefore, graceful leadership requires a great deal of emotional intelligence. We must have both a high degree of self-awareness and a high level of situational awareness. To put it simply, to be a graceful leader, you need to be able to read a room. Graceful leaders establish high expectations for themselves and others, and model those standards on a day-to-day basis.

Graceful leaders show empathy and compassion for others. Rather than accepting excuses, they provide support, resources, and encouragement when others have difficulty meeting expectations. Graceful leadership is a balance between compassion and confidence, care and authority, and humility and poise.

Graceful leadership is as important in the day-to-day work in schools as it is during times of crisis. The most graceful leaders are consistent: they show up at their best during the hardest moments, and they also show up at their best on a regular Tuesday.

Scenario: Graceful Leadership in Action

Imagine that, as a leader new to your school, you begin to have some concerns about the performance of one of your teachers. This new teacher is upbeat and positive with students, shows up on time every day, and interacts well with his colleagues. However, after several visits to his classroom during instructional time, you begin to notice that he lacks effective classroom management skills, that his lesson plans do not seem to be timed appropriately, and the quality of instruction he is delivering is lackluster. There is an overall lack of organization in place, and the end result is that students are missing valuable small group instruction. You know you need to address your concerns with this teacher.

Let's explore the different ways in which a leader might proceed in this scenario. The actions of the principal in this scenario can produce dramatically different outcomes, based upon the leadership style and mindset of the leader.

As the leader in the building, a principal would be well within their place to issue a warning to the teacher, or send an email or memo outlining the areas of concern. The teacher would then have to either comply with the directives or face disciplinary action. He could be placed on a performance plan or recommended for dismissal, based on the word of the principal. This response might speak to leaders who naturally gravitate toward an authoritarian or autocratic leadership style. Responding in this way definitely ensures that the teacher is held to high expectations, but simply telling the teacher he isn't meeting the standards is not likely to help him improve.

Faced with this situation, the teacher might want to comply, but what if he does not have the skills needed to remedy the instructional concerns on his own? What if this teacher is struggling and knows it, and a response like this from his principal might cause him to shut down, and quit? The students would be without a teacher, the teacher would have left the profession, and the principal would need to immediately have a plan in place to provide continuity for students. No one wins in that situation.

Conversely, another leader might opt at this point in time not to address the concerns with this teacher, because surely, there are more urgent problems around the building. The teacher isn't hurting anyone and the children seem to like him, despite the fact that they may not be learning as much as they could be if there were improvements to the instruction in the classroom. This response might appeal to someone with a laissez-faire leadership style.

As in the previous example, if the concerns of the principal remain unspoken, the teacher may still be struggling and know that he needs help. This approach provides him with no support, and worse, could communicate that he is not worth the principal's investment of time, which will likely negatively impact his morale and commitment to his job. The teacher may still ultimately decide to leave if he does not feel effective or supported. Students will continue to miss instruction. The morale of other teachers, who notice a problem that the principal is failing to address, could take a hit. Again, no one wins in this situation.

Now, let's examine how graceful leadership might look in this scenario.

A graceful leader would:

- Neither ignore this issue, nor pull out all of the stops to demonstrate their authority and power as the instructional leader in the building.
- Balance the humanity of this teacher with the communication of high standards, while ensuring that the leader's expectations are backed by resources, support, and encouragement.
- Communicate with this teacher with dignity, respect, empathy, and understanding.
- Prepare thoughtful questions for the teacher that would encourage him to set goals and identify potential resources and supports that would be helpful.
- Connect this struggling teacher with an instructional coach or mentor teacher to engage in collaborative planning or to view a series of demonstration lessons.
- Work collaboratively with the struggling teacher to identify clear, specific goals for improvement and set up a regular opportunity for check-ins to see how things are going.
- Provide actionable feedback to the struggling teacher in a non-threatening way, and encourage the teacher to engage in self-reflection

following lessons to evaluate what went well, and where there are opportunities for improvement.

- Give the struggling teacher the opportunity, space, and time to improve their practice.

Leading with grace in this scenario may still ultimately result in the teacher leaving the profession. Perhaps this teacher would not improve, despite being provided resources, support, and tools. However, unlike in the previous examples, even if the teacher was unsuccessful in improving his practice, he would leave his position with his dignity and humanity intact. He would, hopefully, feel that his principal cared about him as a person, and that he was worth the investment of time and resources. He may choose to remain in education, but pursue a supporting role for which he is better suited. While graceful leadership is not a cure-all solution for everything that is not going well for this teacher, it could make all the difference for him.

The Leadership Lifespan

Any position of leadership is temporary. The length of our tenure as leaders may vary depending on our circumstances. Regardless of the amount of time we sit in a role, that tenure will have a beginning, middle, and end. We will follow a similar arc each time we undertake a new leadership role. I call this arc the Leadership Lifespan.

As school leaders, we can begin a leadership journey at the onset of a new year, due to a promotional opportunity, by transferring to a new position, team, or school as an experienced leader, or when transitioning to a new district. For many of us, we will follow the Leadership Lifespan several times throughout our careers and lives. I have been through the Leadership Lifespan at least five times during the course of my career thus far: as a team leader while teaching, as an assistant principal in two different large elementary schools, as a principal, and as a district-level leader. During the Leadership Lifespan, there are some common experiences we will undoubtedly encounter, including:

- Establishing ourselves as new leaders,
- Facing imposter syndrome,
- Navigating the need for strong communication skills,
- Working with staff with diverse personalities and needs,
- Managing of crises,
- Battling burnout,
- Building a leadership legacy, and
- Transitioning out of a leadership role.

Graceful leadership enables us to remain consistent throughout all phases of the Leadership Lifespan, and the framework of the Leadership Lifespan provides a grounding place for us to keep in mind when we face challenges. As school leaders, on days when it feels more chaotic than calm, we can check in and ask ourselves, "Where am I in my Leadership Lifespan right now?"

It is important to note that the Leadership Lifespan will not always be linear beyond the obvious start and end points. We may pass each stop along the way, but we may also revisit stops during our tenure as leaders, jumping from place to place and back again. As a team leader, I didn't spend much time dealing with imposter syndrome or managing crises, but I invested a great deal of time and energy developing communication skills. When I became an assistant principal, I had my first taste of the nuances and challenges of staffing, but was less focused on building a leadership legacy. The role of principal brought each of the experiences on the Leadership Lifespan to the forefront, and required agility as I often navigated them simultaneously. This has continued in my district leadership role. As a leader, each of the themes from the Leadership Lifespan remain constant for me. Below is a graphic to illustrate the Leadership Lifespan.

Leading With Grace

How To Use This Book

While the book is organized in alignment with common stops on the Leadership Lifespan, you may arrive at different points on your own journey at different times. Therefore, you can move from chapter to chapter in order, or, if it is more relevant to you and your circumstances, you may choose to read chapters out of order. You can also revisit chapters that you have read previously if you need a reminder of some of the tips, or need to reflect and refocus yourself during a challenging time.

Each chapter will start with a personal story, selected to illustrate a leadership lesson that I learned during my time in the principal's seat. Following the story, I will summarize the tips and strategies that I have found personally helpful, before providing questions and exercises for reflection on how you can lead with grace. Because graceful leadership is about being authentic to ourselves, I encourage you to reflect and personalize the lessons that I share in each chapter, and think about how you can implement a suggestion in your own leadership role to further your journey toward graceful leadership.

This book is not intended to be a blueprint, or to be a one-size-fits-all guide. The true value of this book will be in your reflections on the stories, connections to your own life and leadership journey, and application of the tips and exercises in your work. There is no one right way to lead with grace, and no linear path to follow. To truly lead with grace, you must be authentic to who you are.

What Does This Look Like for You?

1. Reflect on the Six Word Story exercise, shared at the beginning of this chapter. Write your own six word story to capture what graceful leadership means to you.

    _____

    _____

    _____

    _____

    _____

    _____

    _____

2. Think of a leader you have encountered in your own life who you would describe as a graceful leader. What qualities and strengths did they possess to make you describe them that way? How did their leadership style have a positive impact on you and others?

    _____

    _____

    _____

    _____

    _____

    _____

    _____

3. In what way(s) are you already a graceful leader? In what way(s) do you know you need to grow to be a more graceful leader?

_____

_____

_____

_____

_____

_____

_____

4. What experience or experiences on the Leadership Lifespan do you currently find the most challenging, and why?

_____

_____

_____

_____

_____

_____

_____

Entering With Grace

"Leadership should be born out of the understanding of the needs of those who would be affected by it."

-Marian Anderson

The First 100 Days

I was promoted to principal in 2019, when I was 37 years old. My own two children were still in elementary school and my husband worked demanding and often unpredictable hours. Fortunately, my husband and I had spent years refining a terrific division of labor in our household, and we were accustomed to juggling complicated schedules and balancing the demands of our family with those of our jobs. I had great support from my parents and siblings, and a community of neighbors and friends who I could count on. As a family, we felt that the time was right for me to make this transition in my career. As a lifelong believer that there is never a "perfect time" for anything, I felt as ready as I could be. I was excited and proud to finally be a principal!

My appointment was announced in early June, and the following day, I was called into my new supervisor's office. I was still riding the excitement from the previous evening's announcement, and relishing this new opportunity. Getting called to the central office so quickly was unexpected. During the meeting, I learned that there were sensitive, urgent issues in the school community that needed immediate and thoughtful attention. The community was highly involved in the school, and while things were running very smoothly in many ways, there had been a series of incidents in recent years that needed to be addressed. Trust was broken between some families and the school. It was going to be no small task to repair what was damaged. I admit, I first felt overwhelmed with the responsibility in front of me. After setting aside my initial feelings of fear about whether I was cut out for the job or not, I jumped in and started working.

As a brand new principal, I was tasked with leading in a high-performing school with a large, veteran staff, many of whom had been at the school for decades. I was the sixth principal some of the teachers and staff had worked for during their tenure at the school. It was a bit intimidating at first to know that many of the faculty and staff had so much experience in the community. I worried that they might not be as invested in getting to know me, having experienced so many leadership changes during their time at the school. My assistant principal was new to the school too, as both previous administrators had retired at the end of the last school year. While my assistant principal was a veteran at the job from his many years of experience elsewhere in the district, neither of us had existing relationships with the staff, students, or community. We both lacked institutional knowledge that we'd come to rely on at our previous schools to keep things running on a day-to-day basis. We were starting from scratch as an administrative team.

As part of the first round interview process earlier that spring, I had been asked to write a plan for how I would get to know my school community as principal during my first few months on the job. To begin to build relationships and establish goals for my first year as principal, I revisited this draft plan as I made my entry. Every single step that I'd outlined in my entry plan was focused on relationships with important stakeholders in my school community. This was my primary focus throughout the summer, and it was where I devoted the bulk of my time and energy. My steps included:

- Developing a strong collaborative working relationship with my assistant principal,
- Meeting with my front office staff,
- Connecting with my custodial team,
- Providing opportunities for optional 1:1 meetings with all members of the teaching and support staff,
- Meeting students and families at a variety of summer gatherings,
- Communicating with principal colleagues at the other schools in our high school cluster, and

- Engaging with community leaders, including our PTA board, local religious leaders, business owners, children's programming staff at the nearby public library, and other community partners.

I'd waited years to achieve this professional milestone, and I had all of the requisite skills and knowledge to do the job. I had high expectations of myself and others, and a strong vision of who I wanted to be as a leader and what I hoped to achieve at my school. However, I knew that I could not come in as a new leader and make changes without building authentic relationships first. I needed to go slowly in order to eventually go quickly. I made it my goal to get to know as much about my school, staff, and community as I could in those first two months before staff and students returned. I needed to truly know the school, including the students, staff, and community, before I established a vision for my time there. Just as kids don't learn from teachers they don't like, adults don't follow leaders they don't know and trust.

My assistant principal and I had both served as assistant principals in the district prior to my promotion. He had also been the assistant principal at my own children's school. While we had a previous collegial relationship and had interacted many times over the years, we did not know one another well. I knew that we needed to build a strong relationship that summer in order to work effectively as an administrative team. As a new principal, I knew what had been most valuable to me during my years in the assistant principal role: being included in decision-making, supported in my own professional growth, and feeling like an integral member of the leadership team. As a result of my experiences, I made sure to include my assistant principal in every opportunity to get to know the staff and community that summer. We met every day during those important first few months to delegate responsibilities, identify who would be responsible for specific tasks that needed to be completed prior to the school year, and to get to know one another better. The trust and camaraderie that we developed during that time allowed us to cement our status as a team.

Over the summer, I hosted informal Meet and Greet opportunities for new students and incoming kindergarteners, and invited all students and families to a "Popsicles on the Playground" event, where the children and families could meet me in an informal setting prior to the start of the school year. Additionally, I scheduled time to meet with the PTA president and board, and connected with several community leaders, local business owners, and the children's programming leads from the nearby public library. I began to meet regularly with the other principals in our high school cluster, learning about long-standing traditions the schools shared.

I sent out a welcome email, introducing myself to the community. In this message, I not only shared my professional background and values, but I tried to insert my own voice into the writing, sharing information about my family and upbringing to build connection with everyone in the community. I also updated our school website to include my welcome message, photo, and contact information. As a result, I began to correspond and connect with families who hadn't been able to attend any of the face to face events we'd offered.

Perhaps the most impactful step I took was to issue an invitation to the entire staff to come in for optional, informal one-on-one conversations throughout the summer. I wasn't sure what to expect when I created and sent out the sign-up sheet, but I was pleasantly surprised to see how quickly the staff took me up on my offer. People came in on their way out of town for vacation, while their families waited in the car, loaded down with suitcases, kids, and pets. They came in between doctor's appointments, and after dropping their kids off at summer camp. The staff planned their valuable time over the summer around coming to school to meet with me. This was one of the first experiences that I can remember where I realized the power of the role of principal. Teachers and staff value one-on-one time with the principal, and when you're new, people are especially curious about who you are and what you are all about.

I learned that summer that often, all it takes to get great feedback and to learn about people, their experiences, and their opinions is simply to take the time to ask. It was extremely touching that people took their personal time during the summer to come in and meet with me, so I not only wanted our chats to be meaningful, I wanted to ensure that they saw action as a result of the feedback they took the time to share. During these staff meet and greets, I asked everyone the same three questions:

1. What do you love about this school?
2. What is something you are open to changing or doing differently?
3. In your opinion, what can I do in my first year to make a positive impact on this school?

Although our conversations were informal, I took copious notes during each and every chat - and I still have those notes to this day. Once I collected the staff's feedback, I spent weeks reading and re-reading the notes, jotting down reflections and identifying common themes in their responses. I even used the commonalities from the staff feedback to create our staff's theme for that school year: Connected, Consistent, and Child-Centered.

As I continued to prepare for the start of the school year, the themes from these one-on-one conversations drove my personal planning - particularly the answers to my last question: *In your opinion, what can I do in my first year to make a positive impact on this school?* I considered it a gift to be told exactly what the staff felt they, the students, and the school needed from me. Because I was new, I could take this feedback at face value without taking anything personally. I committed to making intentional efforts to deliver on what the staff said they wanted from me: excellent communication and a high degree of visibility in order to get to know them and our students.

I took this feedback to heart. I leveraged my strong communication skills to send out a short daily staff bulletin, keeping everyone updated on what was going on around the building and sharing system wide initiatives of interest. I sent a comprehensive weekly community newsletter, corralled frequently used resources in one place within our shared Google Drive, and sent weekly emails to keep staff updated on time-sensitive items. I developed a simple meeting agenda and note taking template that we used across the school for leadership team, committee and grade level meetings.

I also made daily, intentional efforts to be as visible as possible in the building and community. I was a regular presence at arrival and dismissal, greeting students and playing music at the front doors each morning and helping kids into cars at dismissal. I spent hours each day visiting classrooms during informal walkthroughs, and interacted with students at lunch and recess. After visiting classrooms, I made time to leave a quick note or send a short email sharing a celebration or compliment with the teacher. I attended individual team planning meetings, ate lunch in the staff lounge with grade level teachers, and was a presence at every PTA meeting, community event, and extracurricular activity in those important first months. It was a tiring time for this introvert, but it also brought me great joy and satisfaction. These efforts were worth it.

Overall, I felt great about how things were going in my first few months. However, it was important to check in and make sure others thought so, too. I created and administered a survey to solicit feedback from staff after my first 100 days on the job. I began the survey form with a narrative to clarify what my personal leadership goals had been, and to establish how I hoped staff would provide feedback around those goals:

As I reflect on my leadership at this time, I have been thinking about your answers to one of the questions I asked staff this summer during our Admin Chats, "In your opinion, what is the most important thing I can do to make a positive impact this year?" Your answers to this question really helped to form our focus for the year, and I looked through your answers again recently as I thought about how to solicit feedback from you on my leadership.

I have developed a short survey based on your answers to that question this past summer. In our conversations, you told me over and over again about the importance of the following:

- *Engaging the community/parents*
- *Maintaining positivity and building morale*
- *Visibility and getting to know students and staff*
- *Communication*
- *Follow through and organization*

These five themes have been and continue to be a focus of mine. I would love your honest feedback. This survey is anonymous and is so important to me as I strive for growth and to be the best leader I can be for our school. Thank you sincerely for your time completing the survey.

Please use the following scale to rate my leadership in each of the themes listed below. In addition, you can provide open-ended feedback in each area.

1 - Never
2 - Seldom
3 - Sometimes
4 - Most of the time
5 - Always

Thank you so much for your time and honest feedback!

Julia

The questions on my survey were directly tied to the goals I'd set for myself based on those summer meet and greet conversations. Staff had the opportunity to use the numbered rating scale to give feedback on the five focus areas I bulleted above, and after each area, they also had a free text comment box to add anecdotal feedback. At the end of the survey, I included a final question: *Do you have any additional comments to help me continue to grow in my role as principal?*

Truthfully, clicking send on the email with that survey link was scary. I knew I might be opening myself up to criticism, especially with an anonymous survey. I had certainly never worked with a leader who solicited feedback from their direct reports on their performance (and I have never since encountered one). However, I was committed to growth and vulnerability, and felt confident enough in my efforts and in my work ethic to be open to what my staff had to say.

To my delight and relief, the feedback from my 100 day survey affirmed for me that I was delivering on what I'd set out to do. My staff rated me with a score of 5: *Always* 80% or more of the time for each focus area. For three out of five focus areas, 100% of the scores were either 4: *Most of the time*, or 5: *Always*. I only received a total of three scores of 3: *Sometimes* across the entire survey, in the areas of engaging families and visibility.

The narrative comments from my staff were a gold mine. First, they were overwhelmingly positive, which was a confidence boost that I needed as a new leader. Some of the most meaningful comments included "I appreciate how you choose your words wisely and carefully. You make your intentions clear and seem to want to be sure the staff feels supported, while understanding your expectations." and "Continue to ask staff for input when you are looking to make changes. This has made us feel appreciated and has made us feel like we are part of any new efforts you wish to put in place."

One comment that stung a bit when I first read it was, "As a staff, we may have overemphasized the importance of making yourself visible in our classrooms. As much as we enjoy a quick walk-through every once in a while, it can be a distraction to the students and to the staff when we are in the middle of instruction. Sometimes we feel the need to backtrack with the students so that you have some context." Reading it now, it's hard to remember why I took it so personally (it was just one person's perspective on a 100+ person staff!), but at the time, it made me feel unwelcome in classrooms, and I found myself feeling self-conscious when I did my rounds over the next few weeks. To address the feedback, I took the opportunity to share with my grade-level team leaders that the purpose for my visits was to get to know the students, teachers, and instruction across the school, and to clarify that I did not want instruction to stop because I walked in. I didn't need an explanation of the lesson. I also took care to enter and exit quietly, giving a quick, quiet wave to students. When a child wanted to give me a hug or get up to tell me something, I deferred to their teacher and reminded them that I was there to see their hard work.

Perhaps the scariest thing about the deployment of this survey was that I had publicly promised before it was sent that I would publish the results to the entire staff…and after the results were in, I kept that promise. I imported all of the responses, including the narrative comments, into an electronic document. That document was shared with my thanks to the staff for taking the time to complete the survey.

My efforts in the first few months in my school required a tremendous amount of time and emotional energy. I have never worked harder than I did in those first few months. However, the dividends for that initial investment paid off for the next 4.5 years of my tenure there. They continue to pay off today, though I'm no longer at the school, through the relationships I built with staff and the reputation I built across my community and within the district.

Start Strong And Make It Count! Tips for Entering with Grace

1. Get To Know Your School Community

We only have one chance to make a first impression. When entering into a new leadership role, we have an opportunity to establish relationships, set the tone for how we will collaborate with all stakeholders in our communities, and begin to build momentum toward a shared vision.

As educators, our work is people-focused and relational. By choosing to focus on reciprocal relationships - getting to know our staff, families, and students and allowing them to get to know us - we can enter into a new leadership role with grace. In order to truly know those with whom we are working, we have to not only learn about their interests and backgrounds outside of school, we must tap into their strengths in their day-to-day work, as well.

Building a strong leadership team is one of the most important things to do as a new leader. Whether there is an existing group of teacher leaders or a brand new leadership team is being formed, there are many valuable exercises we can use to build community among the team members, identify everyone's strengths and weaknesses, and glean valuable information about the current state of how things are going at the school.

Depending on the size, culture, and needs of your school, your leadership team could range from tiny (perhaps just the principal and assistant principal), to huge (representatives from every grade level team, department chairs, teacher's union building representatives, instructional coaches, student leaders, and even members of the PTA). While I am not arguing for a prescribed number of members or list of positions to include, I do encourage you to evaluate the current makeup of the leadership team at your school and consider how this does or does not align to your needs as a leader. In my experience, smaller leadership teams engage in more efficient decision making. Larger teams provide an opportunity for multiple perspectives.

Personally, I have found that regardless of the size of the leadership team, establishing clear norms around decision making is critical. For example, will decisions be made by consensus, by majority rule, or will members of the team provide input and considerations before a final decision is made by the principal? Making these expectations clear from the outset can ensure all team members are on the same page when discussing items that will have an impact on the entire school. Being transparent around when others will - and will not - get a say in decisions is important for building trust with and among the members of your leadership team.

There are many valuable development tools available, both free and for a cost, that can be used with leadership teams. To explore each team member's preferences for team work, consider using the Compass Points protocol. After time for personal reflection, team members who share common preferences will spend time in small group discussions, before the whole group can debrief on the different styles present within the team. This protocol is simple for team leaders to replicate within their own teams, as well. Principals will not only build a quick understanding of each leadership team member's skills and preferences, they can use this information to match strengths to tasks when delegating work throughout the year.

Make every effort to include all stakeholders in your initial work to get to know the school. Think beyond the leadership team within your staff, including all teachers, paraprofessionals, custodial, secretarial, and cafeteria staff. If there are regular substitute teachers who frequently work in your school, investing time early in building a relationship with them will pay incredible dividends in the future. Consider ways to connect with the parents and guardians in your community. Partner with your PTA to host informal social events, such as a Coffee and Conversation. Visit local businesses to learn about how they may be able to support the school. If your district is supported by a Board of Education, connect with your board representative.

Your district colleagues are another invaluable resource in helping to support your transition into a new leadership role. Other principals in the district in your area or at the same level, your central office supervisors, members of your district's curriculum team, and any professional development specialists are important stakeholders to get to know. Depending on the size of your district, you may even have the opportunity to connect directly with the superintendent to hear about their priorities for your school.

2. Engage In Active Listening

One of the simplest ways that a new leader can learn about their school is by engaging in active listening. Active listening will build trust, encourage others to communicate honestly and openly, and improve staff morale. To practice active listening, be thoughtful about both verbal and non-verbal cues you are sending. Close your computer, put away your phone, and focus on the person with whom you are speaking. Make eye contact and stand or sit with an open presence. Avoid crossing your arms, looking at a clock, or fidgeting. Alternatively, if you know you do not have the time needed to devote your full attention to someone, be honest and schedule a time to follow up with them later.

During my one-on-one meetings with staff, I worked hard to practice active listening. While I did have my computer to take notes, I minimized emails and other distractions. I made sure to explain at the beginning of our meetings that I would be typing to capture their feedback, and did so while maintaining eye contact. I asked follow up questions and suppressed the urge to talk too much myself.

3. Be Visible

It's easy as a new leader to say, "My door is always open." However, we have to recognize that it is critical that we are highly visible in our schools outside of simply communicating an open-door policy. While many staff members, parents, and students will feel comfortable seeking out the principal for assistance or to share a question or concern, others will never take advantage of the opportunity if they feel that they have to find you to initiate a conversation.

Greeting students at the front doors each morning, assisting with car loop or bus duty at dismissal, visiting lunch and recess shifts, and walking the hallways during transition times are easy ways for a principal to be visible throughout the school day. This will not only build rapport with students and staff, it can offer invaluable opportunities to provide just in time support for students and staff members. I found it helpful to use the notes app on my phone when I had an impromptu conversation with a staff member, student, or parent in these settings. This way, I could be sure I wouldn't forget any action items that required follow up later. I have worked with other principals who always carried a pack of sticky notes or a small pad of paper for similar reasons.

Some principals take visibility a step further and forego their formal office spaces for mobile office carts. Others set up work spaces in high traffic areas, such as the school library or in a common area. There are many ways to be visible, but it takes intentionality and thoughtful time management to ensure there are daily, regular opportunities for students, staff, and parents to see and interact with you. Additionally, by getting into as many spaces in the building as possible, you will accelerate the pace at which you learn about the people and structures in the school. I always winced a little when I would pass a teacher in the hallway or staff lounge and they said, "I haven't seen you all week!" To me, that was a cue that I wasn't out and about in the school as much as I needed to be, and that others were noticing.

4. Celebrate Small Wins

A change in leadership sets people on edge, regardless of the strengths and personality of the individual in the role. When establishing ourselves in new leadership roles, it is important to take advantage of every opportunity to celebrate and recognize the positive contributions of others. When visiting classrooms, carry a small pad of paper to jot a quick note of appreciation or to compliment something positive that you observed during your visit. Send a school-wide email at the end of the week briefly highlighting a few celebrations. Build a culture of celebration by getting staff involved. Encourage staff shout-outs through a virtual bulletin board such as Jamboard or Padlet, by having postcards printed and gifting a small stack to each staff member, or by having staff nominate a colleague to be recognized in another special way each week.

Taking time to provide positive feedback pays huge dividends for a new leader. Staff feel recognized, appreciated, and seen. Celebrating small wins builds trust and supports a sense of teamwork in a school. As a leader, you will also get to know others' strengths, which will be helpful in informing your decisions throughout your tenure.

5. Develop An Entry Plan

Identifying attainable goals for your first 30, 60, or 100 days on the job will help you to focus on what is most important in these critical first few months. As a rule, we tend to overestimate what we can accomplish in a short period of time, and underestimate what we can accomplish over a longer period of time. Keep this in mind as you work on your entry plan. If you choose to set goals for a 30 day timeframe, keep them focused and simple. Identify your most important priority for that first month, and do all of your goal-setting in alignment with that priority. For example, if your top priority is building relationships with the staff and community, you might choose to schedule an informal meet and greet opportunity with your students and families and build a sign up sheet for staff to schedule 1:1 check-ins with you.

Equally as important to setting entry goals is making these goals visible to others. Communicate your areas of focus to your staff and community, and consider ways in which you can solicit feedback on how things are going. Develop a simple survey for your staff to complete anonymously to inform you of their ideas about your progress, hold a series of focus groups with parents, or attend team meetings to get feedback from teachers. When you receive feedback, take time for reflection to consider how your actions are aligning with your goals in the eyes of those you serve, and brainstorm ideas for how to continue to work toward your goals.

Entering With Grace - What Does This Look Like For You?

1. Brainstorm a list of stakeholders with whom you can meet to learn more about your school or district. What questions would you ask to help you determine the best path forward in a new leadership role?

    _____

    _____

    _____

    _____

    _____

    _____

    _____

    _____

2. What do you want others in the school community to know about you right away? How can you share this information about yourself in your early interactions with your school community?

    _____

    _____

    _____

    _____

    _____

    _____

    _____

    _____

3. List opportunities for increasing your visibility during and outside of the school day. What is currently getting in the way of your presence during these times? Make a plan to increase your visibility during the times you have identified as in need of attention.

_____

_____

_____

_____

_____

_____

_____

4. What are your strengths when it comes to acknowledging or celebrating others? How can you build a routine around providing acknowledgement and encouragement to your staff?

_____

_____

_____

_____

_____

_____

_____

5. Ask 2-3 people in your school community to describe what they believe your priorities are. Do their answers align with your actual priorities? Do the answers vary among stakeholders? How can you solicit authentic, honest feedback on how your priorities are aligned with your actions?

Facing Imposter Syndrome With Grace

"Imposter Syndrome is a paradox: Others believe in you - you don't believe in yourself. Yet you believe yourself instead of them. If you doubt yourself, shouldn't you also doubt your judgment of yourself? When multiple people believe in you, it might be time to believe them."

-Adam Grant

I Can't Do This!

What I recall most vividly from the days and weeks following my promotion to principal in the spring of 2019 is not the joy of achieving a major professional goal for which I had worked tirelessly for years. Instead, what I remember is the absolute panic that settled over me almost immediately after learning I'd gotten the job. Every time I received congratulations, I smiled, nodded, and engaged in pleasantries. On the outside, I was brimming with excitement. On the inside, I felt terrified. I fought the urge to grab the shoulders of each and every person who wished me well and say, "Help me! How did this happen? I can't do this job! I don't know *how* to do this job! I'm going to fail!" I felt as though I had boarded a high speed train with a one-way ticket to somewhere I wasn't sure I wanted to go.

At the time, I was ashamed to be experiencing these feelings of doubt. I kept my feelings hidden from even my closest friends, colleagues, and mentors. I thought for sure I had made a mistake, but didn't feel that I could articulate how I was feeling to my family and friends in a way that they could understand.

After all, I had excitedly applied for this position, aced three rounds of interviews, and been selected to lead a high-performing elementary school after 14 years working as a public educator. The most I recall saying out loud to others was that I was "overwhelmed", which I hoped conveyed that I was experiencing a wide range of emotions, even though that range was actually pretty slim. These feelings weighed on my mind and my heart around the clock in the weeks leading up to my first day of my new role. I was petrified by the enormity of the position for which I had been selected, and I didn't know if I could live up to the task in front of me.

My story may or may not be unique, but at the time, I certainly felt alone. To me, the idea of speaking to someone about my self-doubt was equivalent to admitting that I was a failure and a fraud. In 2019, I had never heard the term "imposter syndrome", and didn't know how common it was during times of challenge or transition in one's career. I know now that my feelings were driven by a pretty serious case of imposter syndrome. I had worked with many wonderful leaders throughout my career and remembered all of my own principals from my time as a student fondly, yet no one had ever spoken to me about imposter syndrome. Because of this, I was not fully prepared to acknowledge and move beyond these feelings. The negative self-talk in my mind was keeping me up at night. Would I do a good job? Could I really be successful in this role? Was I ready?

Of course, I was able to do a good job! I met with much success in the role, and I was as ready as anyone could be to take on the challenge of the principalship. I worked for 14 years to get this job. I was more than qualified, and received excellent feedback on my readiness from my supervisors, coworkers, and members of my school community. By everyone else's account, I could do this job. Still, the idea of making the transition to the role of principal left me feeling unprepared and out of my depth. I was putting much more weight on the negative self-talk in my head than I was on the support and encouragement I was receiving from those around me. I allowed imposter syndrome to take, and keep, hold over me for several weeks.

During my first few months on the job as principal, I focused on building relationships with my staff, students, families, and community, while leaning on the support of other new principals in my district who were facing the same challenges and feelings. As I grew more and more comfortable in my role, the feelings of self-doubt and the pressure I was putting on myself to be perfect decreased, but they did not go away altogether. The unique challenges of serving as a school leader meant that I was constantly facing novel situations, competing priorities, and complex problems. There were many times during my tenure when I felt that I did not belong in the role of principal, and I truly did walk into the building some days feeling like an imposter.

At this point in my career, I should probably add "expert imposter" to my resume, because in hindsight, I realize that I have experienced imposter syndrome in each and every leadership role I have ever held. I even dealt with it as a classroom teacher! I still recall the feeling of panic that came over me during a pre-service team meeting at the beginning of my fourth year teaching, when I changed grade levels from fourth to first grade. I was embarking upon teaching a primary grade for the first time. This was a change I'd personally sought out to further my own professional growth. At this point in my career, I was beginning to consider pursuing school based leadership. I knew that in order to best support and coach elementary teachers, I would need to truly understand the nuances of both primary and intermediate grades.

My teammates and I were discussing reading plans for the first several weeks of school. Sitting around the table with my colleagues, I suddenly felt overwhelmed with inadequacy at the thought of teaching first graders how to read. My previous experiences in fourth and fifth grades were with students who, by and large, could already read. I was going to have to completely shift my instruction to meet the needs of these younger learners. It obviously was not the first time I'd been made aware that teaching children foundational literacy skills comes with the job of first grade teacher, but it was the first time I'd faced that idea with a feeling of unpreparedness and inadequacy. Hearing my colleagues discuss strategies and use terms that I wasn't yet familiar with made the reality of this change really sink in at that moment. I had a lot to learn, and wanted to do the job well. However, those feelings of inadequacy made me feel as though I wanted to quit and never look back.

Fortunately, my panic was short-lived. I didn't give up - I came back to work the next day, scheduled a meeting with one of our reading interventionists, and became a student again myself. I learned everything I could from everyone who would help me that year. I visited my colleagues' classrooms during my planning time to watch them teach. I had others come in and watch me, in order to gain feedback on how I was applying the instructional strategies I was trying with my students. I tried to be a resource for my teammates, too. I created and shared centers for our students in reading and math, and helped to modify our team's common planning template for small group instruction. I absolutely loved teaching first grade. To this day, that was my favorite year of teaching.

My biggest regret from my early experiences with imposter syndrome is that I kept my feelings to myself. By keeping them a secret, I was unknowingly contributing to the problem. Because I did not talk about these very normal feelings, others around me who may have also been experiencing similar sentiments could have felt as alone as I did. I know better now, and as a result, I am intentionally open and transparent about my feelings when I experience imposter syndrome.

My most recent career change was a pivot from school-based leadership to district leadership. After nearly five years as a principal, I took a leap of faith and transitioned into a district leadership role as the coordinator of recruitment and hiring for my district. I did not have a background in human resources, and I knew the learning curve would be steep. My prior experiences with imposter syndrome prepared me for the change, but no amount of preparation could have completely eliminated feelings of doubt or internal questions about my competence in a completely new role. Based on my previous experiences, I leaned into what I knew well - the needs of our schools, how to effectively manage a team - and prepared myself to be a learner once again. It was still a challenging transition, but I was better prepared than I'd ever been to face imposter syndrome. The tips offered later in this chapter can be used time and again as leaders transition into new opportunities.

Imposter Syndrome In School Leadership

Imposter syndrome, a term that was initially coined to describe an affliction suffered by high-performing women, can impact anyone. However, women, people of color, and other underrepresented groups report experiencing these feelings more in the workplace. Imposter syndrome is defined as the *persistent inability to believe that one's success is deserved or has been legitimately achieved as a result of one's own efforts or skills*, according to the Oxford English Dictionary.

Experiencing imposter syndrome is different than simply feeling a sense of doubt. Doubt is a healthy emotion, and it is normal to feel doubt when working outside of one's comfort zone. We would never experience growth if we didn't have a healthy dose of doubt once in a while. The key difference is that imposter syndrome is persistent and ongoing - it is not a fleeting feeling.

During career transitions, when we accept new leadership opportunities, or even during challenging times as established leaders, feelings of self-doubt and inadequacy can creep in. We may feel as though we have landed a role based on luck, or because we fooled someone into believing we were capable of performing in the position. We may find ourselves attributing our successes to external factors, rather than to our own strengths, skills, and unique abilities. Imposter syndrome can lead to feelings of increased anxiety, and it can have a negative impact on our mental health.

Our interactions with others can exacerbate these feelings, particularly in school leadership. Leading a school is unique. The children are going to show up on the first day of school, regardless of whether or not we are ready, and they're going to keep showing up. There is very little time to prepare for a transition into a leadership role in a school. It is a hard launch. School leaders serve so many different stakeholders, and the need to perform is intense and immediate upon accepting a new role. When new to a school, we are immediately expected to have all the answers, even though we could not possibly do so right away. The pressure to be "on" all the time, to know everything, and to have a solution to every problem can be intense. We must proactively prepare for how to face imposter syndrome so that when it strikes, we are ready. We cannot allow imposter syndrome to go unaddressed.

In her book, *The Secret Thoughts of Successful Women: Why Capable People Suffer from the Imposter Syndrome and How to Thrive in Spite of It*, Dr. Valerie Young identifies five types of imposters. While Young's work was specific to women, the five types ring true, regardless of gender:

- The Perfectionist: this type sets impossibly high standards for themselves, and when they fail to meet their goals, suffer from crushing self-doubt
- The Superwoman/man: this type strives to work harder and longer than anyone else, for fear they will be discovered as a fraud or phony
- The Natural Genius: this type is prone to feeling like a failure if things don't automatically come easily to them
- The Soloist: this type sees the need to ask for help from others as a sign of failure, and would rather suffer alone than seek assistance
- The Expert: this type lives in fear of being exposed as lacking experience or knowledge

I am definitely a Natural Genius type. If something doesn't come easily to me immediately, I experience disappointment and shame. I feel a responsibility to handle things on my own, because to me, asking for help would mean admitting defeat. As a principal, this aspect of my personality was tested in a way in which I'd never been tested before. I needed to develop coping strategies to combat the imposter syndrome that was plaguing me in the principalship.

You Can Do It! Tips For Combating Imposter Syndrome:

1. Focus On Serving Others

We should always remain focused on others, but when we are experiencing imposter syndrome ourselves, turning our attention to students, staff, and families can be especially helpful. You will not only provide assistance or positivity to someone else, you will get a mood boost, which can help to temporarily reduce the negative feelings that come with imposter syndrome. You will also likely get positive feedback from those you are helping, and that will, in turn, help you to restore your confidence in yourself.

Focus on your staff and the instruction they are providing to students by spending time visiting classrooms to intentionally look for opportunities to provide praise. Make sure to leave a note or send a quick email after your visit, providing specific feedback on the positive attributes of that classroom.

Earn a sense of accomplishment by immersing yourself in a task that requires attention to detail and that, when completed, will help staff or students. Sometimes engaging in the simplest of tasks in the building can disrupt negative self-talk. Try something as small as sorting through the lost and found. Folding and displaying the clothes and accessories that have inevitably piled up around the school will help to reunite items with their owners.

Be the talk of a student's dinner table tonight by making a positive phone call home to a family. This will be especially impactful for a student who does not typically get phone calls home for positive reasons. Not only will this improve your mood and make you feel more effective as a leader, as a bonus, you will build a stronger relationship with this family that can endure for years.

2. Practice, But Don't Overprepare

Sometimes, we experience imposter syndrome in anticipation of an important event, presentation, or meeting. Whenever possible, it can be extremely helpful to practice. Before an important faculty meeting, spend time planning your agenda, preparing slides and materials, and setting up the space the day before. If there is a presentation you need to give to a large audience, such as the PTA or a group of colleagues in your district, rehearse.

Preparing notes or even practicing what you would like to say in advance can be valuable when getting ready for a difficult conversation you know you need to have. Make notes or rehearse what you'd like to say when you're alone.

Actors don't get on stage without rehearsing their lines, running through their blocking, and exploring the nuances of what they are trying to convey. The highly visible role we have as school leaders can often feel like acting. By thinking of your practice as preparation to give your best performance rather than "faking it", you may be better prepared to combat imposter syndrome.

One important note when it comes to practicing or rehearsing as a strategy to combat imposter syndrome is to take care not to overprepare. It's important that you do not seem too rehearsed, so avoid writing a script or memorizing verbatim what you want to say. This strategy will be most helpful when you find authentic, just in time opportunities to practice a skill that you want to develop further.

If you can't prepare in advance, try reflecting on a presentation or difficult conversation after the fact. The next time you are faced with this challenge or scenario, you will feel better equipped to deal with it. If you have access to feedback forms, even better. Use the positive feedback from participants to boost your confidence, and reflect on the constructive feedback to improve for next time.

3. Start A "Smile File"

Proactively building and developing your self-confidence as a leader will help you to combat imposter syndrome in the long term. It is important to acknowledge and celebrate your own wins. One way to do this is to maintain a list of achievements in real time. Start a "Smile File" by collecting notes, emails, or even jotting down compliments that you receive from students, staff, families, or colleagues. Keep them in a file folder or box to pull out on days when you are lacking confidence in your leadership.

Get a shout out in the PTA newsletter? Print it! Did a teacher write you a thoughtful note to thank you for something you did to support them? File it! Find a "best principal ever" drawing from a student in your mailbox? You guessed it! Put it in the Smile File to remind you that it is your uniqueness that makes you a great leader! Before you know it, your Smile File will be so full that you'll need to start being selective about what you include due to limited space.

A Smile File will be a useful reflection tool when you need a confidence boost on a particularly difficult day. It can also be a great resource to dig into when preparing for your performance evaluation, too.

When you conquer a new challenge, write a quick reflection, snap a photograph, or capture another artifact to document your success. Especially during your first year in a new leadership role, you will find many opportunities to document what you are learning and new skills you are developing. Being proactive about recording these in your Smile File will help you to effectively brag about yourself at the end of the year to your supervisor, or serve to assist you in preparing for your next promotional interview.

4. Focus On And Grow Your Strengths

Knowing your strengths can help you to nurture them even more, which will make you feel successful when imposter syndrome creeps up on you. Hopefully, you already know your strengths; however, if you need help identifying them, reach out to trusted friends, colleagues, or family members and ask them to list them. There are also great research-based tools and surveys that you may want to explore to guide you to identify and name your individual strengths.

Regardless of your imposter syndrome personality type, you likely value continuous improvement and consider yourself a lifelong learner. Taking continuing professional development courses, joining a professional learning community with other school leaders, listening to education-related podcasts, and reading professional books can all be great ways to keep your skills sharp and pick up actionable strategies that you can implement in your daily work. You will continue to build your expertise and knowledge, which will reinforce your worth during challenging moments.

Facing Imposter Syndrome With Grace - What Does This Look Like For You?

1. When do you feel most like an imposter? Identify the situations that trigger these feelings and write a plan to combat them the next time they arise.

    _____

    _____

    _____

    _____

    _____

    _____

    _____

2. How would you define your strengths as a leader? Create your own list, and ask a trusted colleague, friend, or family member to give you a list of your top three strengths. How does your list compare to the one written by someone who knows you?

    _____

    _____

    _____

    _____

    _____

    _____

    _____

3. Take time to acknowledge everything you are learning in your role. Reflect on the last week, and write down at least three things that you learned. Include your list in your Smile File.

_____

_____

_____

_____

_____

_____

_____

_____

Communicating With Grace

"Communication sometimes is not what you first hear, listen not just to the words, but listen for the reason."

-Catherine Pulsifer

The Positive Shout Out From an Unlikely Source

One year, as a staff appreciation initiative, I created an electronic form for parents to complete to share positive feedback to teachers and staff. Like most principal colleagues I knew, I was always on the hunt for inexpensive ways to foster positive morale among my staff. Teachers are always much more touched by a thoughtful note or email from a family than any tangible gift, so I built this initiative around that idea. We called it the "Staff Shout Out". Families received a basic Google Form with directions for the staff appreciation initiative. The text from the form is included below:

This week is Employee Appreciation Week throughout our district. We are showing our appreciation for the outstanding people who make a positive and lasting impact upon the lives of our students each and every day at our school.

We wanted to extend our families an opportunity to join in on the fun. We encourage our families to take a moment to recognize a staff member who has made a positive connection and/or impact upon your child and/or family. Feel free to submit this form multiple times for different staff members. We will share your message with each individual staff member. Thank you, families, for the outstanding support and encouragement you always show our staff!

I monitored the responses as they came in, forwarding the feedback in an email to the individual staff member who received the shout out. Below is an example of one parent's acknowledgement of her daughter's second grade teacher:

Mrs. F is such an amazing teacher! She's always so creative with her rewards systems in her class, which has made such a positive learning environment for her students! She recognizes the students both individually, and as a class. The students are constantly earning their rewards, which is a testament to the classroom community she has created. Mrs. F's care for her students is so evident in the detailed messages she sends home. Parents greatly appreciate her weekly emails where she highlights the positives of the week and acknowledges the achievements of her students. We are beyond grateful for Mrs. F!!

Sending emails to each staff member who received a shout out form was the highlight of each day during that week. Teachers responded to the emails, or stopped by my office, to tell me how much it meant to have even one sentence of encouragement. I was pleased with the response from families and the positive impact it was having on staff.

One morning several days after launching this initiative, I logged in to view the new responses. I began scanning through the recent entries, copying and pasting the messages into emails and firing them off to the appropriate staff members. I was working in a good rhythm and was almost caught up on that day's responses when one particular shout out stopped me cold. It was written by a parent with whom I'd had the single most negative interaction that entire school year - and it was for me!

Earlier in the school year, I had to call this parent to inform her that her child would be required to quarantine due to potential exposure to an individual who tested positive for Covid. It was the winter of 2021, and in our district, we were engaging in contact tracing each and every time a member of the student body or staff tested positive for Covid. I hated making those calls, because parents were never happy to be on the receiving end of one. Most parents at least understood and acknowledged that I was doing my job, and despite their disappointment with the situation, were kind and civil to me.

This call was different. This parent screamed and cursed at me over the telephone for nearly half an hour because of her frustration with this policy, which required her child to stay home from school for five days to isolate. She called me a robot. She accused me of lying about her child's "alleged" exposure to a Covid-positive person, and she demanded that I reveal the name of the person with whom her child had contact. When I would not reveal any identifying information, she threatened to call the superintendent. She peppered her castigation with profanity. I felt so demoralized during that call, but remained professional and polite, right up until she hung up on me.

I remember so vividly how I felt at the end of that call. Her words were biting, and it felt personal. Her tone with me was sarcastic and demeaning, and left me feeling disrespected and deflated. While I knew that her frustration on that call was actually with a policy, not with me, it certainly did not come across that way in the moment. I was a human being to whom she could direct her frustrations. The negative feelings I experienced when I hung up the phone stuck with me for the rest of that week. It was several years ago now, but I can still hear the scathing tone in her voice. It really stuck with me.

I should note that in hindsight, I should not have allowed that call to go on as long as it did. In the moment, I froze, and like her, I was tired and emotionally drained from over a year of leading my school through the pandemic. On that call, I felt that it was my job to take the abuse. If I had the opportunity to live through that call again, I would handle it differently. Our district had a civility policy, and I should have leveraged it and calmly ended the call as soon as she started cursing. On the other hand, if the call had gone differently back then, I might not have this story now.

If you'd told me at the time of that phone call that just a few months later I would be on the receiving end of a positive shout out from that same parent, I would most certainly have laughed. If I was asked to define her opinion of me based on that single communication, it was clear that she did not value me as a partner in her child's education, or respect me as a leader and a human being. I really thought she hated me. I would have believed you if you'd told me she had a dartboard in her basement with my face on it! Yet, when she saw the message about our staff shout out initiative, somehow it was me who she chose to recognize! She took the time to complete our online form - to give *me* a compliment! Her comment was:

(This shout out is for) Mrs. Bialeski, for enduring an incredibly challenging year, and having the hard conversations with parents throughout the ever-evolving pandemic.

Her comment shocked me, and I never would have expected her to think of me with respect based on our phone conversation earlier in the year. I am embarrassed to admit that I spent a great deal of time - for weeks after our interaction - ruminating over her opinion of me. I relived our conversation numerous times, as I walked my dog, washed dishes, and drove to work. She had obviously gotten under my skin, and worse, I was feeling as though I was in the wrong, when in fact I had just been doing my job making that phone call. I was sure that it would be so terribly uncomfortable to look her in the eye the next time we saw one another. None of that mattered to anyone but me. I was taking her communication so personally, I was losing sight of the big picture. Ultimately, receiving this shout out affirmed for me the importance of always leading with grace, particularly during tense and trying times. I came out on top, despite her verbal tongue-lashing. After all, I hadn't done anyone wrong in the first place!

To this day, I don't know whether that parent even remembers our tense telephone call. More than likely, she was letting off steam and releasing her frustrations on me, because the situation left her feeling helpless. I was her target because I was taking the time to listen. I was a human to whom she could direct her anger about the pandemic and its impact on her family. The impact of that communication on me was much greater than it was on her. By receiving that shout out form, I learned an important lesson not to take negative communications to heart. I wish I could go back in time and tell this to myself as I hung up the phone with her - it would have saved me more sleepless nights than I care to admit!

Communication In School Leadership

There is really no undervaluing the importance of excellent written and oral communication skills in school leadership. As principals, we must regularly engage in both proactive and reactive communication, serving a diverse audience, all of whom have different preferences about how and when they like to receive communication. Striking the perfect balance is impossible, and there will always be some stakeholders for whom your communication is either too much or not enough. Marrying your communication with strong interpersonal skills is imperative, too.

Proactive communication is used to share important information in advance with stakeholders. School newsletters, back to school mailings, and even phone calls can be used proactively to reach out to families. An example of proactive communication with staff might be a summer back-to-school email in advance of staff returning to the year, packed with schedules, introductions of new members of the staff, and information about what to expect during any in-service days.

One-on-one proactive communication is just as important. From the first line of an email, letter, or phone call, we can begin to forge strong relationships between the school and community. For example, I started each and every parent phone call by first assuring the parent that their child was fine and safe, because I knew that getting a call from the principal might lead some parents to assume there was an emergency. Initiating a call or email with a family or staff member "just because", to check in and see how things are going, can open - and maintain - the lines of communication.

One proactive communication step that brought me great joy was sending each and every newly enrolled kindergarten student a handwritten postcard over the summer, welcoming them to our school. I also did this for any first through fifth grader who was new to my school. As a child, receiving mail was so exciting for me, and to this day, I love a handwritten note! I took advantage of the quieter days over the summer to write a handful of postcards per day, tracking which students I'd written to in our internal enrollment document. I kept a packet of blank postcards and a roll of stamps in my work bag, so that I could jot a few lines and drop a postcard in the mail wherever I was when I found myself with a few minutes to kill. The amount of positive feedback that I received from kids and parents, based simply on a couple of sentences on a postcard, was tremendous. During our kindergarten play dates over the summer, parents would stop me on the playground and tell me how much the notes meant to their child.

One parent told me that her daughter kept my postcard on her nightstand, and that she would find her sometimes "just gazing at it with a smile on her face". I will never forget that! The image of that sweet five-year-old holding my postcard as if it were a treasure stayed on my mind for weeks after hearing that story! Taking time to proactively reach out to students and families is an investment that can pay huge dividends in the future.

Reactive communication is a necessary evil as educational leaders. We will inevitably find ourselves in situations where we need to communicate with a quick turnaround, possibly with only limited information available. When leading schools, it's not if something will go wrong, but *when*. Because our business is children, and they are the center of everything we do, there is a different level of urgency and importance to the way in which we communicate than in other professions. Trust and transparency are key while communicating in schools. A graceful school leader understands that word spreads quickly in a school community, so when there is important information to share, it should be shared as transparently as possible.

While I have always considered myself a good communicator, in my first year as a principal, I saw how much value my responsiveness held for my school community. The job is, of course, much more nuanced and complex than simply being responsive, but for many stakeholders - parents, especially - there are very few times when they reach out directly to the principal. The impact that the principal's responsiveness can have can be immense in these cases. Though it may be a singular experience, a parent can hold on to that impression of you forever as a principal who promptly helped them through a challenging situation. That parent may never need to reach out to you again, and therefore the impact of that one small interaction can be great. To put it simply, being responsive leads to positive relationships. People learn that they can count on you to address their concerns, answer their questions, and provide them with the information they need. Being responsive communicates respect.

You Can Do It! Tips For Communicating With Grace:

1. Personalize And Vary Your Communication

As school leaders, we must be able to communicate with many different audiences. Students, parents, community members, staff, and district colleagues all need to understand our message. As such, it is important to avoid educational jargon, and to review and edit our communication to ensure we are choosing the most straightforward way to communicate our messages. At the same time, our communication should be genuine, and should reflect our own unique voice as a leader.

Before sending out written communication, ensure you have proofread your writing, and consider having another staff member review it to make sure that your message is clear and that your writing is grammatically correct and free of typos. Nothing will undermine your message more than the discovery of a typo by a member of the grammar police! Depending on the demographics in your community, you may need to have your written communications translated into languages other than English before they are sent. In some districts, there are dedicated staff who support these efforts, but if your district does not have translation resources, Google Translate can work in a pinch.

People are busy, and we have access to information with more frequency and volume nowadays than ever before. Therefore, a graceful leader must err on the side of overcommunication to ensure that everyone receives a message. Leverage all of the tools at your disposal, including email messages, social media, your school's website, automated phone calls, hard copy letters and fliers, and face-to-face reminders in order to communicate with staff, students, and community members. Identify and take advantage of opportunities when many parents and families will be visiting your school, such as parent teacher conferences, performances and concerts, or even in the car drop-off area before and after school to connect to and communicate with people. One of the best purchases I made for my school was a large, foldable sandwich board with a weather-resistant cover. We used it in the car loop in the mornings and at dismissal to remind parents about early dismissals, special events, and deadlines. Our busy community appreciated a quick, easy reminder that was right in their faces at the moment they needed it!

When possible, pick up the phone. A phone call is a personal way to communicate with families. This can be a great way to share happy news, issue a personal invitation to a hard-to-reach family to increase their participation in school events, or to defuse a tense situation. Sometimes, email is not the best way to go when you know a situation is delicate. Regardless of the reason for the phone call, a best practice is always to follow up on the communication in writing, so that all parties are on the same page. Our district's student management system included a communication log feature that was useful in documenting phone calls and in-person meetings. Any member of the staff could summarize a communication for all other colleagues to access at a later time.

2. Avoid The Responsiveness Trap By Establishing Communication Boundaries

While responsiveness has many benefits, there are definite pitfalls of being too responsive as a school leader. We can easily become trapped by our own responsiveness. This was a challenging lesson that I learned early on in my time as a principal. I was so stuck on the idea that responding immediately to each and every email and phone call I received, or pausing what I was doing to answer a staff member's question, made me a good communicator. As a result, I fell too easily into the responsiveness trap. The more responsive I was, the more others expected me to be available to them. If I replied to an email within the hour, the next time, someone would expect me to respond even sooner. If I was unavailable to take a phone call or to speak with a parent who had stopped into the office with a question, it seemed as though I was failing to communicate. Whatever I did, it never seemed like enough. I needed to learn to manage expectations around communication - my own and others'.

I began to use technology to my advantage, leaving non-urgent emails marked unread in order to set better communication boundaries and remain focused on other tasks throughout the work day beyond simply replying to emails. I also took advantage of the "schedule send" feature in our email platform. This way, I could immediately respond to a question while the answer was fresh in my mind, but delay the timeline in which the sender received the response. This was also helpful if I chose to reply to emails outside of regular work hours. I found it helped with maintaining professional boundaries when families didn't grow to expect a response from me late at night or over the weekends and holidays. After employing these strategies, I noticed that staff and families reached out to me less frequently on evenings and over the weekends, yet they still received responses to their emails in a timely fashion.

Another pitfall of the responsiveness trap is that when you become too responsive, some stakeholders will begin to come to you with questions that could easily be answered by others. Instead of calling the front office, visiting the school's website, or using Google, they will begin to come to you first, because they know you will reply. As a school leader, you have more important priorities than answering these types of questions. Just because you are able to answer, that does not mean that you should answer.

When I found myself stuck in this trap, I would respond, but would clearly direct the person with the question to the correct source of the information. For example, one year I noticed that a PTA board member had gotten into a habit of emailing me every time he wanted to know whether there was mail in the PTA mailbox. There were many other staff members who could have assisted him with this basic question. He could have called the office, stopped by the school, or reached out to one of his fellow board members to see if they had picked up any mail that was addressed to him. After receiving this question a few times, I politely responded by copying my secretary and asking him to call the front office for this information in the future. Then, I stopped replying to those inquiries.

3. Don't Take Things Personally

A wise friend of mine once told me that when she is feeling anxious or finds herself perseverating on a negative interaction with another person, she gives herself an important reminder: No one is thinking about you as much as you think they are. Hearing those words from her hit home for me, and they have given me valuable perspective in my journey as a leader. If I had heeded that advice after the call that I described in the story at the beginning of this chapter, it would have saved me hours of stress.

Most of us know that the majority of the time, someone's failure to communicate in the way in which we wish they would is not about us. In the moment, it can be difficult to be cognizant that it isn't about us. When you have a tense interaction with a parent, a difficult conversation with a staff member, or you are frustrated with someone else's lack of responsiveness, remind yourself to QTIP - Quit Taking It Personally. It's likely not about you. Because of this, always strive to take the high road when communicating. Conduct yourself with grace, communicate respect and empathy, and take comfort that the conflict you are experiencing is not personal and is not a reflection of who you are as a leader.

This tip still challenges me, and if you are also a natural people-pleaser, it might challenge you, too. Keeping some reflections in a journal or even in the notes app on your phone can help to remind you in the moment about all of the other times when you took something personally that you shouldn't have.

4. Embrace Two-Way Communication

It can be very easy as a school leader to miss opportunities to engage in two-way communication. Practice active listening by maintaining eye contact, avoiding distractions from your computer or phone, asking questions, and jotting notes while the other person is talking if that will help you to synthesize information. By listening to understand, you will be able to best help resolve a situation.

When I first became an assistant principal, I felt tremendous pressure to solve every problem that was shared with me. I found myself listening for the purpose of developing a solution. Every time a teacher came to my office to share a problem, I immediately clicked into solution-mode.

As a result, I didn't always engage in active listening. I was too busy thinking of ways to solve the problem that I wasn't thinking critically. Additionally, not everyone will come to you expecting you to solve their problem. When I began to realize I needed to improve my active listening skills, I started asking the question, "What do you need from me in this conversation?" Often, teachers and staff would share that they just wanted to vent. At other times, they did want to engage in problem-solving with me. Knowing the goal of the person with whom I was communicating ahead of time helped me to listen more actively.

We must also remain open to feedback from all stakeholders, including staff, families, and even students. There are many ways to engage the school community in two-way communication. Forming staff and student advisory committees, holding recurring informal opportunities for parents to engage with the administrative team, such as monthly Principal's Coffees, maintaining a standing open agenda during PTA and faculty meetings, and using an old-fashioned suggestion box are all ways in which school leaders can solicit feedback from all stakeholders. Ultimately, modeling active listening and making others feel comfortable sharing concerns and questions with you will have the biggest impact on a culture in your school where feedback is valued.

Communicating With Grace - What Does This Look Like For You?

1. List the types of proactive communication you currently use. Identify a gap and brainstorm how you can improve your proactive communication.

   _____

   _____

   _____

   _____

   _____

   _____

   _____

2. What could you do to improve your active listening skills? Identify 2-3 action steps you can take to be a better active listener.

   _____

   _____

   _____

   _____

   _____

   _____

   _____

3. Reflect on the story from the beginning of this chapter. What is the biggest lesson you have learned about communication in your own experience as a school leader?

_____

_____

_____

_____

_____

_____

_____

4. Have you ever fallen into the responsiveness trap? What tip from this section of the chapter resonates with you and why?

_____

_____

_____

_____

_____

_____

_____

Staffing With Grace: Recruiting, Hiring, Managing, And Retaining Staff

"I am convinced that nothing we do is more important than hiring and developing people. At the end of the day, you bet on people, not strategies."

-Lawrence Bossidy

Every spring, after receiving our preliminary staffing allocations for the upcoming school year, I would embark upon several weeks of frenzied interviewing for vacant positions. In a typical year, I was primarily working to fill support positions: paraeducators, student assistants, and secretaries. Unlike some of my colleagues at other schools in our district, I rarely had teaching vacancies in my school. We had a fairly low turnover rate for teachers, due in large part to our geographic location, which was close to two neighboring counties where many teachers in the district lived. Our school made for an easy commute for those coming in from the neighboring counties, and we had a good reputation among teachers for being a great place to work. Our families and students were a large part of that reputation, too. Our student enrollment was consistent from year to year, so we did not often see an uptick in the number of teaching positions allocated to us by the district. In many ways, it was wonderful to have low turnover. However, this also meant that I only had rare opportunities to select teaching staff. Every chance to hire a teacher, then, was that much more important, and I felt a lot of pressure to get it right with every hire.

My school housed two regional special education programs: an Academic Life Skills program for children in the elementary grades, and an early childhood center for children who were preschool and prekindergarten age, which we called the RECC. Our RECC had existed when I arrived at the school, but the expansion of prekindergarten in Maryland had brought further growth following the pandemic. We started with two RECC classrooms at the time I arrived at the school, and had added a third the previous year. This year, we were adding an additional two classrooms, which would each be co-taught by a special educator and general educator. This meant a significant expansion of our staff.

For this particular school year, I would be hiring three teachers, and several paraeducators and assistants to support the children across the program. Selecting teachers and staff who would help to grow the program while contributing positively to our school culture was paramount. The early childhood center had long operated as a "school within a school", and the staff and families reported that they did not always feel included in the overall school program. The staff did not see themselves reflected in the professional learning amongst their colleagues, and did not feel that they were consistently given a voice in school-based decisions, from the master schedule to special events. It was important to me to address their concerns with the expansion of the early childhood center, and hiring the right people was an integral step.

In the post-pandemic era, our district had maintained virtual transfer fairs, where teachers and staff who had submitted to transfer within the district to our school could meet with our team for an informal interview. These virtual meetings were akin to speed dating, with only ten minutes to meet with a prospective staff member via Google Meet. Ten minutes is not a lot of time, and therefore every second counted in order to both evaluate if the candidate would be a good fit for our school, and to sell ourselves to teachers who we hoped to woo. To prepare, I perfected a quick elevator speech about our school to open these meetings, so that I could leave the majority of our precious interview time to the candidate.

I agonized over selecting the right questions to ask of the candidates. I needed to strike a balance between gauging their knowledge, skills, and abilities as an educator, while also leaving the interview with a sense of who they were as a person. The RECC required a highly collaborative team, because each classroom contained several adults working side-by-side throughout the day to support the children. These were our youngest students, and many had learning challenges. For these students, who were toddlers during the pandemic, coming to our school would be their first experience away from home and their first opportunity to socialize with peers. I needed staff who could effectively manage student behavior, create authentic, trusting relationships with parents, and collaborate with colleagues both inside and outside of their classrooms.

Additionally, for every position I interviewed, I felt it was important to get a sense of the candidate's personality and character. We had invested significant time as a staff engaging in a collaborative process to create a shared vision for our school. I wanted to be sure that each new hire would be invested in that vision. How would they respond to interpersonal challenges or react in the face of a crisis? What would they do when faced with an ethical dilemma? Would they be willing to have a difficult conversation with a colleague if it meant making the best decision for kids? The answers to these questions were far more important to me than whether someone had effective classroom management skills or could follow a lesson plan. I could teach someone those skills if I needed to. I couldn't teach them to love and care for children if it wasn't already a part of who they were.

To prepare for interviews with prospective special educators, general educators, paraeducators, and assistants to join the program, I wrote and revised interview questions several times. I sought input and feedback from the team leader, before landing on the questions below:

- What experiences and qualities do you possess that make you highly qualified for a position in RECC, and why do you want to be in this position?
- In the RECC, our team is highly collaborative and flexible, and we value the contributions of our temporary employees, student assistants, paraeducators, related service providers, and teacher colleagues. Please speak to your experiences working with colleagues within your classroom in these roles.
- Describe how you would respond to a student who is having difficulties with behavior in your class.
- How will you empower parents and community members to become part of our students' learning experiences at the RECC?
- Think of a challenging situation or change you have encountered as a teacher, and describe how you overcame the obstacle.
- Describe your experiences providing academic support to students within and outside of the classroom.
- As you are assisting one of your students who is having difficulty in the hallway, two staff members walk by and make a comment about the student you are working with. What do you do?
- At our school, we are committed to serving our diverse students and community by providing a safe, inclusive learning environment for all

students, and removing barriers to ensure equitable access for all. Tell us about how you would support these efforts in your role.

I tailored the specific questions that I asked from this list to the role for which I was interviewing. All candidates answered the first and last questions, which gave them an opportunity to share their professional background and unique skills that led them to seek out the position at our school and speak to how they saw themselves in our school's vision. Teaching candidates received the next four questions, and paraeducator and assistant questions received the final three. The end result after a whirlwind round of interviews was a selection of staff who we knew could not only effectively teach and support our student population, but would be able to contribute positively to our overall school culture.

For potential employees who I knew would be highly sought after at many schools, I invited them for a school tour following the virtual interview. I knew that I could do my best to convince them to call our school home if I had the opportunity to meet them in person, show them our campus, and speak with them informally as we walked the halls. On these visits, I took them to the classrooms where they would be working so that they could envision themselves in the space. I introduced them to their potential teammates, to the front office staff, and to other colleagues as we moved throughout the building. I shared a bit about myself not only professionally, but personally, talking about my family and personal interests as we strolled the hallways. Every candidate who I invited for a tour that year ultimately selected our school.

Of course, interviews are just one part of the staffing process. For the purposes of this chapter, I will be addressing staffing as it pertains to recruiting and hiring, managing, evaluating, and retaining staff. The story above speaks to the recruiting and hiring process. The tips in the next section will address all four components.

Tips For Staffing With Grace

1. Execute The Recruitment And Hiring Process With Intentionality

Interviewing

As a leader, it is critical to be purposeful and intentional during every step of the recruitment process when you have positions available at your school. From the moment you identify a vacancy at your school, begin thinking about the process you will use to identify the best candidate. This includes writing thoughtful interview questions, considering who you will engage in the selection process, when you will schedule interviews, and how those interviews will be structured.

Ideally, you should convene a diverse panel for interviews. Your panel can consist of staff who are familiar with the work of the role for which you are interviewing as well as parents, and in some cases, even students. While there may not be a perfect panel size, aim for a total of 5-6 people. As you identify people to serve on the panel, consider whether all candidates will be able to see themselves reflected in the panelists. Strive to form a panel with diversity of experiences and backgrounds as well, so that many different perspectives are present when debriefing candidates after interviews. Ensure that prior to starting interviews with the panel, you review the questions and scoring protocols with them, and emphasize the need for confidentiality throughout the interviewing process.

If you have many applications for a position, your interview panel could be engaged to review resumes, cover letters, and any other information you have about applicants prior to scheduling interviews. This will help to narrow the field of candidates and identify the best qualified applicants to invite for an interview.

Once interviews are scheduled, it is important to consider the experience that the candidate will have from the moment they arrive. If your interviews are in person, is there a quiet space where they may be able to take a few minutes to review the questions prior to coming in for the interview? This is a great strategy that sets the candidate at ease, and allows them to put their best foot forward in the interview. Offer bottled water, a pen, and a notepad for the candidate during the interview. Think about how you will open and close the interview: what information do you want to convey about the role for which the candidate is interviewing and about your school? In today's job market for educators, it is incumbent upon leaders to sell themselves and their schools just as much as the candidates must sell themselves. In the face of nationwide teacher shortages, candidates often have several choices, and as a leader, it is your job to make sure that if given a choice, a top notch candidate will choose you and your school.

Onboarding

Once you have hired someone new, think about how to best welcome that person to your school. Onboarding new teachers and staff is an invaluable opportunity to welcome, support, and ultimately retain staff. This is a time to foster a sense of belonging for new staff. It is also an opportunity to convey your expectations, provide resources, explain the evaluation process, and connect new staff to mentors. The actions you take as a leader at the beginning of a staff member's tenure at your school can pay great dividends in the future of this person's success.

As soon as a new staff member accepted a position at my school during the summer, I would send them an email, which served to welcome them and to provide early resources to help them feel connected to our school and ready for the upcoming year:

Welcome to our school!

First, we want to officially welcome you to the staff! We are so thankful that we will be working together.

I joined this school community in July 2019. Throughout the last three years, despite the many challenges and hardships that were brought about during the COVID-19 pandemic, I learned firsthand that our students, staff, and community are amazing. You will love it here! I am thankful that you have decided to join our staff and look forward to the contributions you will make to our school community. We are going to have a great year together!

The assistant principal and I are both here to support you this summer, and if we don't see you before August, we can't wait to hear about your adventures during your well-deserved time off!

Here are a few things I'd love for you to share with us as we plan for a great opening in August!

1. *Complete the Staff Shirt Sizes form so that we can order you some staff spirit wear this summer!*
2. *Save the date for a New Staff Welcome luncheon in the Media Center on the Friday before staff return. This will be a casual get together for us to meet and for you to meet other new colleagues, and lunch will be provided. Please let me know if you are able to attend.*
3. *Please email me the following information to include in our "Meet the New Staff" slideshow. These slides will be shared with our staff during our welcome communication in early August, and will be shared with our community as well.*
   a. *A photo of yourself*
   b. *A brief 2-3 sentence bio*
   c. *2-3 fun facts about you*

If you need anything at any time - have a question, want to share a picture from your summer adventures, or just want to check in - I can be reached by email or you are welcome to text or call me on my cell phone.

I would also like to introduce you to our Teacher Development Liaison (TDL). He is copied on this email. He will be a great resource for you this year as you join our staff, whether you are a veteran or new educator. He will be partnering with the administrative team in August to help welcome you formally and bring you up to speed on all things related to our school. Additionally, he will be able to support you through the evaluation process next year, whether you will be on- or off-cycle as a teacher or support staff member.

We can't wait to see you soon!

Leverage other veteran staff, such as instructional coaches, team leaders, and other members of the administrative team to check in with new staff members in their first weeks and months at the school. Starting a job in a new place can be overwhelming, and it is important that new staff do not feel alone. They should have many places to turn with questions or to access resources. Connecting new staff with veteran staff is a great way to not only build positive relationships among staff, it is a way to build the capacity of your existing staff in mentoring and coaching others.

2. Master Performance Reviews

Provide Regular Feedback

In education, performance reviews are more than a once-a-year exercise. Provide your teachers and staff with regular feedback on their work. Giving regular feedback does not have to take an inordinate amount of time. Make use of opportunities to give quick feedback on sticky notes or pre-printed cards as you walk through classrooms. I ordered a large pack of blank postcards with encouraging sayings on the front from Amazon, and kept these in multiple places - on my mobile office cart, in my desk, and in my work bag. When I saw something I wanted to recognize, I jotted a quick note and left it on a staff member's desk or in their mailbox in the front office. It didn't take long, and was a great way to encourage more of the positive things I was seeing from that person.

Do your best to ensure that every member of your staff receives informal feedback regularly. I tried many different strategies to keep track of my efforts to provide feedback to staff over the years. One year, I kept a separate file folder for each staff member. I would file a copy of an email, note, or formal observation write up into the folder throughout the year. By the end of the year,

I had several artifacts in the folder for that staff member that I could use to inform my evaluation report. This strategy worked well for collecting evidence in one place, but was too complicated to be effective for me. I found that taking the time to print emails or make photocopies kept me from other tasks, and I still was not equitably providing feedback to staff across the building. At the end of the year, some staff members had several artifacts in their folders, while others may have only had one.

Another year, I created a spreadsheet with every staff member's name listed alphabetically in the first column. I started at the top of the list, and my assistant principal started at the bottom of the list. We challenged ourselves to visit at least five classrooms per day, with the intention of providing the teacher with specific feedback about what we saw. We kept a log on the spreadsheet of who we'd seen, and because we each started at a different place, we didn't duplicate efforts. This worked well for getting to each and every member of the staff in a strategic way, but did not work as well for collecting feedback in one place centrally that we could refer to at a later date.

In my final year at my school, I created a Google form that was tied to our school improvement plan goals, and set up condition rules so that we could evaluate our goals in language arts, math, and school climate on the same form. My assistant principal and I each bookmarked the form on our phones, so that we could quickly complete it as we visited classrooms. In our staff bulletin each Monday morning, I announced that week's instructional focus, so that staff knew what we would be looking for as we conducted our classroom visits. I shared the look-fors in advance, so there were no secrets about what I expected to see. I'd complete the form right on my phone as I moved throughout the school. Then, I could email a copy of the responses to the teacher immediately following the classroom visit. If I happened to miss the instructional focus during my visit to a classroom, I would complete as much of the form as I could, and offer to come back at a later time. This often led to great discussions with teachers about what they were doing instead during the time of my visit, and gave me an opportunity to come in again a day or two later to see the part of the instructional block I'd missed.

I found great success with this strategy. It not only allowed me to track where I had been by exporting the form responses to a spreadsheet (one of my favorite features of Google forms!), it gathered the data in one place, which was terrific to have when it came time to evaluate our school improvement plan goals at scheduled intervals during the year. Finally, this strategy worked well since I could immediately provide teachers with feedback without delay - often before I left their classroom. On the opposite page is an example of the feedback form that a first grade teacher received by email, immediately after my walk through in her math class:

Math Feedback

23-24 Math SIP Statement of Commitment:

Teaching staff will consistently analyze actionable data to differentiate during first instruction.

Name of Walk Through Tool*

Elementary Mathematics Instructional Walkthrough Tool - Number Routines

Number Routines

These effective teaching practices are adapted from Principles to Action (NCTM, 2014) and align with trauma informed instructional practices.

Type of Routine*

Number Talk

Number Talks Specific

The following Number Talks specific look-fors were observed:*

✓ Used an appropriate Number Routine (The routine was either a Number Talk or a routine from the grade level mathematics curriculum)

✓ Engaged students in sense-making (Students had the opportunity to think and reason before ideas were shared)

✓ Facilitated meaningful discourse (Discourse featured student voice and ideas anchored by think-pair-share and other discussion techniques)

✓ Established an environment for a routine (Students are in close proximity to the teacher and one another to promote student-to-student discourse.)

✓ Solicited and investigated multiple solutions (Multiple answers are solicited before multiple strategies are recorded and discussed)

✓ Recorded student thinking accurately (Teacher records multiple student strategies accurately and clearly)

✓ Focused discussion on efficiency and flexibility (While different strategies are accepted, discussion helps students see that certain approaches are more efficient than others. Discussion also helps students see how strategies are related resulting in the same solutions to help them move between strategies when possible.)

Compliments and Considerations*

First of all, it is so obvious that you have invested significant time this year establishing the routine for Number Talks in your math classroom. Your students know the signals, and are confident in responding to one another's thinking.

I noticed that you solicited multiple answers before facilitating a discussion around strategies. You reminded students multiple times about the language you want them to use (respectfully agree/disagree). You rocked it! Great work.

Engage Staff In Goal-Setting

The start of the school year is a terrific time to engage in goal-setting. For goal-setting to be truly productive and effective, rather than just a box to check, it should be a collaborative process driven by the staff member. In most districts, this endeavor can be aligned with the evaluation system for staff. In our district, teachers were evaluated using the Danielson Group's Framework for Teaching. Teachers in their formal evaluation year were required to select a component from the Planning and Preparation and Principled Teaching domains to focus on for the year. Our support staff, including paraeducators, student assistants, and secretaries, were evaluated using a performance review tool with rubrics for professionalism, job knowledge and skills, interpersonal skills, and relationships with students and families.

Consider providing a guidance document for staff prior to holding goal-setting conferences at the beginning of the year. Outline the requirements for performance evaluations, including the timeline for any conferences, observations, or submission of professional artifacts. Allow staff to reflect on their personal goals for the year, and consider using some guiding questions to get them thinking.

I was able to use the existing structure of our evaluation system as a roadmap for these goal-setting conversations. If your school or district does not have a resource that you must use, consider external tools. Engage staff in writing SMART goals - goals that are Specific, Measurable, Achievable, Relevant, and Time-Bound. The University of San Diego offers a free template and several examples of SMART goals for teachers, if you need inspiration.

Take Formal Observations Seriously

Teachers take their formal observations seriously, and as a leader, you should too. In my experience, I found that being formally observed was consistently stress-inducing for many teachers. As an instructional leader, it is important that you maintain the integrity of the formal observation process, while also remaining attuned to the vulnerability that teachers experience when someone is coming into the classroom to watch them in action.

Before The Observation

From the outset, communicate your expectations with teachers about what you are looking for during the observation. While I had many principal colleagues who chose to forego pre-observation conferences due to time constraints, I never did. A teacher will likely have a very different experience planning for and executing a lesson if they have an opportunity to engage in a conversation about their learning objectives and the needs of their students with their administrator than if they simply plan on their own. I utilized the time during my pre-observation conferences to set the tone for teachers, by sharing my personal philosophy as an observer. My first goal was always to come in and lift up the positive things that I saw in the classroom. I wanted teachers to know that I was not looking for an opportunity to catch them doing something incorrectly; rather, I was looking for an opportunity to highlight a strength that they may or may not have realized they had. I was always clear that if there were concerns, I would be open about sharing them, but framing my intention prior to the observation in this way helped to put teachers' minds at ease as they prepared. As a result, they were in a more relaxed state during the lessons and would deliver their best instruction.

While a formal pre-observation conference will not be possible while conducting unannounced observations, it is important to convey your philosophy about the observation process to your staff at some point. This could be done at the beginning of the year during a faculty meeting, during a special meeting with staff in their formal evaluation year, or during individual goal setting conferences at the beginning of the year. You can also start your post-observation conferences by spending a few minutes sharing your overall philosophy in order to frame the conversation in a positive way.

During The Observation

There are many demands on an administrator's time, and sometimes, canceling or rescheduling a scheduled observation with a teacher might be inevitable. Take caution not to allow this to become a habit, however. Teachers put an incredible amount of work and time into planning for these lessons, and showing up when you are supposed to communicates respect for their time and energy. To minimize disruptions, I would coordinate observations with my assistant principal's calendar. This way, one of us was always available to handle emergencies, while the other was conducting a formal observation.

When in the classroom for an observation, take copious notes. If you are a fast typist, train yourself to transcribe what you hear, so that you have direct quotes from the teacher or students to refer to when analyzing the lesson. Engage with students if you are able, to ask them about what they are learning or to listen in on their discussions. During transition times, make notes of the things you see around the classroom that are informing instruction, such as what is written on anchor charts, how the learning objective is displayed for students, and even the physical setup of the classroom.

At the end of the observation, take a quick moment to give the teacher a piece of immediate feedback. Because being formally observed can be a stressor for teachers, it can mean a great deal to get a quick compliment once the lesson concludes. I would send a brief email to the teacher before I left their classroom, thanking them for having me and highlighting one or two positive attributes from the lesson. I would always end by telling them that I looked forward to discussing the lesson in more detail during our post-observation conference. Those quick emails meant a lot to my teachers.

After The Observation

Following an observation, make time within a day or two to meet for a post-observation conference. Allow the teacher to kick off the conversation by reflecting on how the lesson went, identifying any opportunities for improvement, and articulating next steps in instruction for this group of students. Plan thoughtfully in advance for these conferences by jotting down some strengths you observed, and a question or two for the teacher.

If you have concerns about instruction, classroom management, or anything else that you observed during the lesson, be particularly thoughtful in planning how to share this feedback during the post-observation conference. Do not avoid addressing concerns, but be sure to think through how to best share the feedback with the teacher, including what supports and resources you can offer to help them improve. Providing critical feedback without an offer of support or any suggestions for how the teacher can improve will not lead to positive outcomes. Is there a mentor teacher or colleague who excels in the area in which this teacher needs assistance? Arrange classroom coverage so that this teacher can observe their colleague in action. Do you have an instructional coach who might be able to co-plan with the teacher to assist them in enriching their instruction? Make sure to thoughtfully pair resources with the area of need. Then, if possible, offer to come back and provide feedback after an identified period of time to help the teacher monitor their progress in the area of need.

Retain Your Best People

Retention is critical when it comes to staffing. A graceful leader will take intentional actions to retain strong teachers and staff. According to a Learning Policy Institute (LPI) report released in 2017, there are four key factors that impact teacher retention: compensation, teacher preparation, administrative support, and working conditions. In most cases, a school leader will not have the ability to control compensation and teacher preparation. However, a school leader can have tremendous influence over administrative support and working conditions within their school.

According to the LPI report, teachers who do not feel that their administration is supportive are twice as likely to leave the profession as teachers who do feel that their administration is supportive. In other words, a supportive principal can be the reason why a teacher chooses to stay. Maintaining positive relationships with teachers is paramount in helping them to feel supported. Putting the tips into practice which were presented in Chapter 2 regarding active listening, visibility, and celebrating small wins are great ways to encourage a culture where teachers feel supported by the administration. Chapter 6 will delve deeper into supporting teachers during challenging times, and the tips in Chapter 7, which focuses on preventing burnout, will also support a culture where teachers feel supported.

As a leader, you have a tremendous impact on the working conditions within your school. Teachers should have access to the materials and resources they need to do their jobs, while having the time needed to plan for students. The decisions you make as a leader can make or break the working conditions for your staff.

While you may not be able to create more minutes in the day, you can help to build a schedule that maximizes those minutes. Protect teacher planning time and ensure that when building the master schedule, teachers have time throughout the week for collaboration with colleagues. Think beyond the minimum number of minutes that may be required in your teachers' contract. Just because you can schedule a meeting doesn't mean you *should* schedule a meeting. Giving teachers agency over their time is one of the most impactful choices you can make as a leader.

Utilize funds to provide instructional materials to support teachers, and partner with community organizations, such as your PTA, to provide teachers with financial assistance for out of pocket costs for their classrooms. Seek input from teachers when planning for professional learning sessions, whether it be a faculty meeting or a full day professional day.

Work with your custodial team and district to keep your physical facility in good shape. Teachers, staff, and students spend the majority of their waking hours in the school building, and if something is dirty, broken, or in disrepair, it can have an impact on everyone.

Above all, be relentless about building and supporting a positive school culture. Happy teachers work hard. People who love coming to work tend to have good attendance at work. When staff feel supported, heard, and encouraged, they are invested in remaining at a school, and in the profession, for the long term.

Staffing with Grace: What Does This Look Like For You?

1. Think about your current approach to interviewing for vacant positions at your school. Identify one action step you can take to best position your school as a top choice for candidates during the interview process.

    _____

    _____

    _____

    _____

    _____

    _____

    _____

2. How do you currently conduct pre- and post-observation conferences with teachers? List 2-3 questions you might ask in your standard pre- and post-observation conferences. How would you plan for a post-observation conference with a teacher about whom you have performance concerns?

    _____

    _____

    _____

    _____

    _____

    _____

    _____

3. We know that working conditions have a significant impact on teacher retention. Identify one action step you can take toward improving working conditions in your school, and make a plan for this improvement.

_____

_____

_____

_____

_____

_____

_____

_____

Managing Crises With Grace

"Keep your fears to yourself, but share your courage with others."

-Robert Louis Stevenson

On March 13, 2020, I called a brief staff meeting before school. We called these "stand up" staff meetings, because they were reserved for last minute announcements or quick updates, and were meant to be so brief that everyone could remain standing. I'd invited our PTA president to join us. I will never forget standing up in front of my staff that morning in our media center. It was a Friday morning, and I'd been summoned with all of the other principals in my district to a meeting with the superintendent the previous evening. An evening gathering of the district's 78 principals together on a few hours' notice had never been done, but the circumstances we were facing were most unusual.

Once everyone was assembled, the energy in the room was tense. I could see that people were nervous and uncertain, based on their facial expressions. My own heart and mind were racing, but I knew that I was standing in front of people who were looking to me to lead them through a crisis. My job was to remain calm, be a steady and positive presence, and to reassure the staff that everything would be okay - even though I was not feeling all of these things with confidence. Regardless of my own personal feelings, my job was to provide my staff with the facts that were available to us, communicate what I needed them to do, and be there for support. I needed my staff to be in an emotional space to support children in just a few minutes when the bell rang for the day. I was 8 months into my first year as a principal, and was still getting to know my staff, students, community, and finding my footing in my new role. The situation I was facing was truly unfathomable.

My announcement that morning did not take anyone by surprise, as the afternoon before, our governor had announced an emergency two-week closure of schools due to the emerging COVID-19 virus. I informed the staff that they would be off for the next two weeks, suggested that they check email periodically for updates to this developing situation, and spent the remainder of the meeting time encouraging them to be a caring, calming presence for children all day. Instruction was to continue to normal, and any students who were worried or expressed anxiety would have access to our student services team. The district curriculum team had worked literally through the night to prepare instructional packets for the students to bring home, and our logistics team had prepared and delivered hard copies to the school. Kids were to bring home their personal belongings at the end of the day.

Once students arrived, the day itself was eerily calm, despite the circumstances. I spent much of the day checking in on staff and students, answering logistical questions (Should we send home their pencil boxes? Who will clean out the refrigerators? What do we do from home for the next two weeks?), monitoring updates from the central office over email, and responding to questions from parents. At the end of that day, we sent students home with their belongings for what we believed would be two weeks. I threw my computer charging cord in my bag, and as an afterthought, loaded the plants I kept in my office into my trunk so they wouldn't have to go without water for two weeks.

My first few days working from home were incredibly busy. I set up my kitchen table with my laptop and a notebook, because our home did not have a formal office space. My husband is a first responder, which meant that I was flying solo at home with my own two elementary-aged children. In those early days, I was getting my first taste of what turned out to be five months of juggling working full time from home while attending to the needs of my family. Additionally, like everyone else, I felt uncertain not just about what this emerging pandemic meant for me professionally. I was also personally scared. In those early days in the spring of 2020, we were learning more every day about COVID-19. Local businesses were announcing closures by the hour, grocery stores were like the wild west, and none of us knew what else was to come.

Staff and parents were reaching out to me at all hours of the day and night. These two stakeholder groups had very different needs early during the school closure. For most of my staff, their questions and needs were largely logistical. There is a common personality type drawn to working as an educator. Educators are detail-oriented by nature, many have a "Type A" personality, and we are used to working with a high level of organization and advanced planning. Something like this completely threw many staff members, who were not accustomed to this unprecedented level of uncertainty. Staff were calling, texting, and emailing to ask questions, many of which were very specific, "What if?" type questions, for which I simply did not have answers.

The communication that I had with parents during the pandemic school closure followed a very different trajectory than that with staff. For the first few weeks, when we were still operating under the assumption that we were closed for two weeks to contain the spread of COVID-19, I received messages of support and encouragement from parents. Families wanted to remain connected and in communication. I began recording and emailing out daily video morning announcements from my living room. In the videos, I shared a joke of the day, talked about what I would prepare for dinner, and chatted as though students were able to respond to me. My children or dog often made cameos, and sometimes I wore silly glasses or affected an accent. I gave students birthday shout-outs, and shared photographs that students had emailed to me. At first, these video morning announcements provided a way for our students, parents, and staff to remain connected with me. As a newcomer to the school, many families loved seeing me in my home, interacting with my children, dressed down and being silly. I got great feedback from parents and students.

As things with the pandemic progressed, it became clear that schools were not going to reopen after two weeks. The calls and emails from parents shifted from words of encouragement and reactions to the daily morning announcements. Our parents and caregivers grew more panicked. In some cases, parents were directing their anger and frustration at me, and their communication was hostile in nature. Everyone was struggling to determine how they would continue to work with their children at home. Some families were facing financial strain due to loss of work. Stress was high all around. Parents joined staff in looking to me for answers. The pressure was on.

This was my first experience managing a crisis as a new principal, and a worldwide pandemic had certainly not been on my bingo card when I accepted the job! I quickly realized that my role as principal was especially critical during this time. As principals, we know that our job is to lead a school community, but in a crisis situation, we are needed in ways we may not have expected.

My experience as a new principal during the onset of the pandemic was formative in many ways. This was the beginning of my crash course in carrying "the weight" of the role of principal. The idea of this "weight" of the job is the most consistent piece of feedback I have heard time and again from school principals, regardless of their background, years of experience, school level, or district. The weight that came with being a first year principal during the pandemic was incredibly heavy, and I had no roadmap or blueprint to follow. No one else could coach me through this experience.

I have often likened making the transition from assistant principal to principal to becoming a parent for the first time. When I was pregnant with my oldest child, I read books, took parenting classes, and talked to friends and family members who had been through this experience before. I bought baby gear, interviewed pediatricians, and set up a nursery. I had, quite literally, thousands upon thousands of hours of experience with children. I could easily envision myself as a parent. I was excited to love my baby, prepared for sleepless nights, and could imagine our new family when this little person finally arrived. I had done all of the research and preparation that I thought possible, but still, when my son was born - in the very first second - an entire part of my heart and mind opened up that I didn't even know was there. I held my baby and thought *Nothing could have prepared me for this!* At the same time, something inside of me clicked and I realized, "I get it." I understood in that first moment that I held my son what I'd thought I understood before, but had never personally experienced. I understood that the love for my child was unlike any other feeling in the world.

Stepping into the role of principal was like that for me, and the crisis of the pandemic shortly thereafter amplified this feeling. At that time, I had 14 years of experience in public education, serving as a teacher, instructional specialist, and assistant principal. I had worked in four different schools in two different districts. I had central office experience. I'd worked with, learned from, and grown under six different principals over the course of my career. In my years as an assistant principal especially, I had gained experience in all aspects of running a school. Cerebrally, I knew exactly what the job of a principal looked like. However, I didn't fully understand what that responsibility - that weight - would feel like until I was actually in the role. Managing a once in a lifetime crisis during a global pandemic in my first year was not at all what I thought I signed on for.

We cannot prepare for a crisis in advance. Once one hits, we have no way to know how long it will take to resolve. The pandemic started as a two-week school closure, yet in the end, it took years for my school to return to a sense of normalcy. The ripple effect that one crisis can have on students, staff, and community members is immense. While difficult to do, leading with hope, authenticity, and resiliency during a crisis can be incredibly formative for a school leader. We should not underestimate the power of graceful leadership during challenging times. For me, I found my confidence and grew into my leadership style when I had to lead my school community through this crisis.

The pandemic is an extreme example of leading through a crisis, but as school leaders, we frequently encounter crises, both large and small. Additionally, depending on an individual's definition of the word "crisis", sometimes we are called upon to navigate a situation that to some, constitutes a major emergency, while to us, it may not feel like a big deal. The tips in the next section will serve school leaders during a crisis of any scale.

Tips For Managing Crises With Grace:

1. Get In The Pond

One day, a nonverbal student, who was newly enrolled in our academic life skills program, ran away from the playground. This student was an extremely fast runner, and we were still getting to know his preferences and learn how to best support him. Within seconds of his elopement from the playground, he was knee deep in the water retention pond on the side of our building. As an aside, this particular pond, like most water retention ponds in the mid-Atlantic region of the United States, was composed of approximately 90% goose poop and 10% water.

When the call came over the walkie talkie, I acted as I always did when I knew a child or a staff member was in trouble. I took off down the hallway at full speed, in my high heels and a brand new dress. About halfway down the hall, I kicked off my heels so that they wouldn't slow me down (or cause me to break an ankle) once I got onto the grass outside. I rounded the corner of the building by the pond, just as a teacher was leading the student back to the building. I was fully prepared to throw my new dress directly into the trash can upon re-entry to the building. Any principal worth her title keeps a change of clothes at school for such emergencies!

I never actually made it into the pond, but it was clear to every staff member who saw me running, and to those who heard about it later, that I was prepared to jump in. Later that evening, I started receiving texts from colleagues at other schools, who had heard the story - but in the version they'd heard, I actually did get in the pond!

The lesson that I hope this story illustrates is that as a leader in a crisis situation, you must always be willing to do the dirtiest, least desirable job. Even the fact that I was going to get in that pond brought me instant credibility and respect with my staff, and even with administrator colleagues from outside of my school.

When a crisis arises, big or small, take an opportunity to put yourself in the least desirable spot to manage the problem. Even if it means literally getting your hands (or new outfit) dirty. If, both every day and during the most difficult times, you model that nothing that needs done is beneath your title, your staff and community will follow suit in troubled times.

During a crisis, school staff are often called upon to go above and beyond the call of duty to support students and families. This might mean working longer hours, being available at a moment's notice to provide support to someone, dealing with a physical cleanup, engaging in fundraising or donation collection efforts, and more. When you are at the front of these efforts as a leader, it sends a strong, powerful signal to your staff and community. They will follow your lead. Because you cannot singlehandedly manage a crisis, it will be critical to have buy in and support from your staff and community.

2. Control The Chaos

In times of crisis, people panic. It's human nature. In schools, it is imperative that adults model calmness for children (and for one another). As school leaders, we can help to manage the emotions of others in several ways. Whenever possible, pull staff together in person to share information, such as during an informal, brief meeting before or after school. Having all staff together in-person provides you with an opportunity to disseminate information to everyone all at once, despite the fact that you may not have had the opportunity to create a slide deck or plan and print a formal agenda. Preparing a bulleted list of talking points in advance can be helpful to manage your own emotions and stay on message as you share the necessary facts with a large group of people.

Just as it is normal human behavior to panic during a crisis, it is also common during uncertain times for people to engage in speculation. People naturally want to make sense of things, even when they don't make sense. This can result in many "what if" questions, or even the circulation of rumors. Rumors and "what ifs" do not contribute to a sense of calm, however. Be transparent with facts, and be explicit with staff that you are sharing everything that you know with them. Ask them directly not to engage in gossip or indulge in speculation, even if they feel the urge to do so. Assure them that any updated information will be communicated to everyone as soon as it is available.

After any in-person meeting, follow up in writing with a summary of what was shared, any action items necessary, and a recap of your expectations. As emotions will be running high during a crisis, people will not be able to retain all of the information that you share orally. As the situation develops, continue sending memos or brief updates through email, so that everyone stays in the know and has the information they need to continue to tackle the crisis situation.

3. Check In On People… And Take Care Of Yourself

During and after a crisis situation, leaders must offer processing time to people. Students, staff, parents, and community members have different preferences and needs when it comes to processing difficult situations. As leaders, we must lean in to our emotional intelligence and remain attuned to how those around us are doing. This means that, in addition to offering space and time for people to process, we also must provide follow up support as necessary.

When managing a longer-term crisis, schedule regular, predictable check-ins for people to bring questions, debrief challenges they have faced that week, or just have face time with you as the leader. During the pandemic, when our staff were working remotely and our district had to pivot to virtual instruction, I held weekly virtual office hours for staff during our shared lunch period, and weekly virtual principal's coffees where parents could drop in to ask questions. These informal opportunities provided valuable time for me to connect with the community I was serving, and they were a predictable time for our stakeholders to have questions answered and concerns addressed.

Depending on the specifics of the crisis, you may need to check in individually on specific students or staff members. Perhaps a particular class, grade-level team, or school bus was impacted by a crisis. Identify the additional needs that this group may require, and create a plan to get those supports in place. Think beyond your own skills and abilities in crisis management. If your district has a crisis team, this is a great time to leverage this resource and bring in experts to assist you. Other local government agencies, non-profit organizations, or even houses of worship in your community may have resources to offer to help staff, students, and families process a crisis.

Your role as a leader during a crisis is invaluable. To do your job at your best, you must also make proactive efforts to look after your own feelings while you are focused on taking care of everyone else. Ensure that you are getting enough sleep, eating properly, and processing your own feelings. Leverage mental health resources available to you through your district's employee assistance program or through your health insurance plan. Find a trusted friend outside of work in whom you can confide. By taking good care of yourself, you will be able to more effectively lead others through a crisis. Taking care of yourself as a leader will be explored in more detail in Chapter 7.

4. Model Hope, Adaptability, And Honesty

Above all, during a crisis situation, others are looking to their leader, and they are watching and listening at all times. How you carry yourself during challenging times will be remembered long after the difficulties have been conquered.

Maintaining a sense of hope is paramount during a crisis, whether it is a short-term emergency or long-term challenge. As a leader, you can model and instill hope in others. If there is something that can be done to make progress toward recovering from the crisis, or even just to improve the current state of things in your school, identify specifically what can be changed and communicate that with staff, students, and the community. When we feel as though we can take actionable steps to make something better, it gives us hope and brings back a much needed sense of control during uncertain times.

Adaptability can be the difference between simply surviving through a crisis and coming out better on the other side of a crisis. While remaining resilient allows us to bounce back once a crisis is resolved, being adaptable means that we move our schools and communities forward as a result of challenging times. As leaders, we can model adaptability by actively seeking out ways we can improve processes during a crisis to best support our communities, and then build upon those process improvements once the crisis is resolved. We can model being the lifelong learners we so often say that we are by engaging in real time professional learning with our staff to better cope with challenges.

Even in "normal" times, we can model adaptability in order to maintain a mindset of flexibility and growth in our schools. Often in schools, students, staff and families become comfortable with the "way things are done". By challenging ideas, practices, and structures that may no longer be best serving students and the school community at large, we can model adaptability in advance of challenging times so that when a crisis arises, adapting to any changes that it brings will feel more comfortable for everyone.

Honesty and transparency are critical during times of crisis. As a leader, people must be able to trust that we are telling them the truth, even if the news is grim or not what they want to hear. We must be honest, decisive, and clear in our communication. It can be challenging to address concerns directly, or to communicate the truth without providing a false sense of hope. However, failing to communicate honestly can lead to the spread of misinformation, as well as eroding trust. Once people lose trust in a leader, it is extremely difficult to rebuild.

Communicating with transparency is important following a crisis as well. Meeting with your crisis team and debriefing a situation provides everyone with an opportunity to learn from this situation and be better prepared for the next challenge. If something didn't go well, or you realize that you handled a part of the management of this crisis poorly, be vulnerable and own it during the debrief with your team. Share what happened, what you would do differently in hindsight, and how the crisis may have been managed more effectively. Our crisis team was composed of the administration, school counselors, school psychologist, pupil personnel worker, nurse, health assistant, secretaries, and a few hand-picked teachers who had strong logistical skills and who I trusted would remain calm in the face of challenges. Our team would debrief after every emergency drill as well as in real time during a crisis situation. Together, we were able to identify strengths and areas for improvement, gauge how our staff and students were feeling and deploy resources to support those who needed it, and problem-solve to improve our response the next time we faced an emergency.

Following the debrief, communicate with your larger stakeholder audiences. When planning for follow up communication, consider timing, the visibility of the crisis, and confidentiality. For example, when our elementary school was evacuated shortly before the end of the school day due to a small fire in the kitchen, we knew that students would immediately report the incident to their parents when getting into the car or off of the bus. It was important to me that families received an email from the school prior to hearing the news from their children for the first time. This incident was highly visible, as it impacted all students and staff, and the location of our school on a heavily trafficked road meant that some members of our community had seen fire trucks on the property when driving by that afternoon. There was very little need for confidentiality in this situation, because no students or staff members were directly impacted.

We decided to be as specific as possible in our email to parents, informing them that the school was evacuated due to a small fire in the cafeteria kitchen. We explained that the fire originated in the dishwasher, and that students were not present in the cafeteria when it started. We shared that the building was immediately evacuated, emergency personnel responded quickly, and gave the length of time students were outside while the firefighters were assessing the situation. As a result of this proactive communication, my assistant principal and I received zero parent phone calls or emails that evening about the incident.

Ultimately, there is no one right way to manage a crisis, and every situation is unique. However, if you show others you are willing to "get in the pond", control the chaos, check in on others, care for yourself, and model hope, adaptability, and honesty, you will be able to effectively lead others through challenging times.

Managing Crises With Grace: What Does This Look Like For You?

1. Reflect on a crisis that you have faced in your current role. What did you do well during that time? What would you do differently if faced with this situation again?

_____

_____

_____

_____

_____

_____

_____

2. How would you project positivity and hope for others during a crisis situation? Brainstorm specific methods of communication and strategies you would use to lead with grace during a crisis.

_____

_____

_____

_____

_____

_____

_____

3. Think through how you would remain attuned to the needs of your staff, students, and community during a crisis situation. What strategies would you use to check in on people? How would you know when someone needed additional support?

_____

_____

_____

_____

_____

_____

_____

_____

Battling Burnout With Grace - Bringing Your Best Self By Prioritizing Your Wellbeing

"Give up the delusion that burnout is the inevitable cost of success."

-Arianna Huffington

The Importance Of Disconnecting

On the day that school closed for winter break in December 2022, I practically had to drag myself to my car in the parking lot when it was time to go home. For months, I had been physically working at school for nearly ten hours a day. I was connected to my phone when I wasn't at school, responding to calls and text messages from staff and replying to parent emails at all hours. Yet somehow, my to-do list remained never-ending, regardless of how long I spent at work. I arrived home cranky each night, and was quick to snap at my family. I felt capable of little other than collapsing onto the couch as soon as I'd kicked off my shoes in the evenings. I was burning the candle at both ends just to feel as though I was barely keeping my head above water. I was mentally and physically exhausted, and as a result, I was not performing at my best at work or at home. I felt like a failure. I was so dejected, I began to question whether I could remain a principal, or if I even wanted to remain in the field of education.

It was especially frustrating for me to find myself in this position, because well-being is, and always has been, a core value of mine. I was doing so many of the right things: getting enough sleep, eating well, exercising every day, meditating, leaning on friends and family for support, and yet, I still found myself experiencing burnout. I was not only tired, I was living in a way that was out of alignment with my values, and that was worse.

I went home that evening and made a small but actionable decision: I was not going to check work email at all over the coming ten day winter break. I set up an automatic reply on my email, logged off of my computer, and shared my plan with my family members. My husband was cynical and not sure that I could actually follow through on what I intended to do. My kids, however, brightened immediately at being asked to help keep me accountable. They were happy to be a part of my goal, even though they may just have been excited at the prospect of catching me red handed on my computer. Spoiler alert: they didn't catch me. I stuck to my goal and did not check email once over that break. There may not be anything revolutionary about putting on an automatic response while out of the office and staying off of email during a break, but for me, it was the first time I had done so in over a year.

The result of this action step was that at the end of that winter break, I felt more rested and relaxed than I had in a very long time. I felt ready to return to work and hit the ground running, and I couldn't believe how restorative those ten days had been for me physically, mentally, and emotionally. I vowed to myself that I would find a way to carry some of that energy with me into the new calendar year by setting better boundaries between work and home.

What did I miss by staying off of work email for ten days? The truth is, not much. Granted, it was a quiet time of year, since schools were closed, but upon my return to the office, my inbox was primarily cluttered with spam and automated notification emails. Upon checking my inbox on January 2, I had one moment of regret. Out of all of the spam and other inbox clutter, my decision to stay off of email did result in missing one important piece of information. Over the break, a pipe in my school had burst, causing flooding in a few of our classrooms on the first floor. The district's maintenance team was immediately alerted, and they had been working for several days on cleanup and repairs. Our district's protocol did not include calling the principal of the building, so the only communication about this incident on which I was included was an email chain. Because I'd missed the emails, I missed the chance to send out a message to staff, preparing them for what they might find when they returned from break. Our occupational therapist's motor room was hit the hardest by the damage, and she came into work on January 2 to a mess. The building smelled of mildew and there was a lot of cleanup to do, despite the fact that our spaces were usable.

If I'm being honest, my initial instinct when I read about the flood was one of panic. I felt I'd made a huge mistake by staying off of work email. I was so tempted to undo the progress I'd made over the break and revert back to my old, bad habits, even though I knew they were not serving me well. Instead, I took a moment and really thought through how I was feeling - and why I was feeling that way.

I knew that I was experiencing guilt, due to feeling that I let my staff down by failing to prepare them for the mess following the flood. On the other hand, I knew rationally that the majority of my staff were disconnected from work over the break too, and would not have seen an email from me even if I'd sent one. Most of those who *would* have seen a message would have logged on first thing that morning before leaving for work. I realized that had I spent the break connected to email, the reality is that I would have given some people a heads up of a *couple of hours* about the flood. The positive impact on them wouldn't have been very significant. The impact on my mental health of staying disconnected from work over the break, however, had been incredibly significant. This reflection helped me to keep my values in perspective.

Following that break, I certainly couldn't ignore email forever. That would not have been reasonable or feasible. Maintaining a work-life balance does not mean that work gets ignored in the long term. What I chose to do instead was to set a time for myself each day after which I would not check email for the rest of the evening. I also vowed to stay off of work email over the weekends, unless an emergency arose that required my attention. This strategy worked well for me, because I respond well to clear, solid boundaries. Other people might do better with boundaries that are less clearly defined, but I needed the hard and fast rule of "no email on weekends". For several months afterwards, I kept a list of the occasions when an emergency happened that required me to log on to my computer. The final list fit on a 1x2 inch post-it note.

Over the remainder of that school year, I continued to reflect on the impact that this small tweak to my work-life balance was having on my well being. Personally, I felt more present at home for my family. I was less stressed, I had more patience with my children, and I found myself smiling and laughing more at home. Most surprisingly, though, was the positive impact that this boundary had on my professional life.

Somehow, I found that being less connected to email resulted in my feeling as though my work was *more* manageable. Because I was taking a nightly break from thinking about and attending to work, I was then able to be more productive, thoughtful, and calm during the work day. By allowing my brain to shift out of work mode when I was home, I brought my best self to work each day, and I was a better leader as a result.

I have often described myself as a recovering people-pleaser. Making other people happy has always been important to me, and throughout my career, as I moved into leadership positions, this need to please others initially showed up as a constant, self-imposed pressure to be responsive. As a new leader, I felt that the way to lead best was to model that I would never stop working until the work was done. My work ethic was a personal point of pride, and I never wanted to be caught resting. Even in my personal life, I spent weekends making to-do lists and felt a sense of accomplishment when a weekend ended and everything on my list was checked off. Eventually, I learned the hard way that working, or even just thinking about work nonstop, would only lead to burnout. I wasn't functioning at my full capacity.

Further, I realized that modeling an unhealthy relationship with work was doing others who were watching me more harm than good. How could I suggest to a member of my staff that it was okay to shut work off at the end of the day if I never did? What message was I unintentionally sending about my expectations for them if I was emailing at all hours of the night? I also became aware of the example I was setting for my children. Did I want them to grow up to believe that they weren't working hard enough if they wanted, and needed, time to themselves?

While I expected a positive result for myself from taking a break, I underestimated the power and influence that my boundary reset would have on my staff. I shared the story of my experience with burnout during faculty meetings, with my instructional leadership team, and during one on one conversations with staff throughout the school day. The response was immediate. As I shared my story, I noticed tears in the eyes of some of my teachers. One teacher stopped me in the hallway several days later to thank me for my vulnerability, because hearing me say that I was going to be working less in the evenings and on weekends made her feel that it was okay for her to do the same. She didn't need my permission, of course, but she felt inspired to follow my example and take positive steps toward better work life balance.

It was, and remains, uncomfortable for me to truly rest. However, knowing that protecting my own time was contributing to a culture of better balance for my staff gave me motivation to stick to my goals, even when I felt tempted to slip back into old habits.

Work-life balance is constantly in flux, and to attend to it, we must regularly check in and evaluate how things are going and adjust accordingly. As school leaders, our work has seasons. The beginning and end of the year might require more time and attention at work, while the middle of the year and the summer may be less busy, and the needs of our lives outside of work might be more time consuming. If we continually evaluate our boundaries and rebalance our time, we will be more likely to avoid burnout.

Tips For Finding Battling Burnout With Grace

1. Minimize Decision Fatigue With Habits And Routines

Leading a school requires you to make hundreds, if not thousands, of large and small decisions every day. The American Medical Association defines decision fatigue as *a state of mental overload that can impede a person's ability to continue making decisions.* According to a 2016 Wall Street Journal article by Jim Sollisch titled The Cure for Decision Fatigue, the average American adult makes 35,000 decisions each day. When I was a principal, I began making these decisions for my school from the second I woke up in the morning. Who would cover for the teacher who texted overnight to tell me that they were taking today off? How would I respond to the angry parent who would be waiting in the office first thing this morning to talk to me about an incident that occurred on the bus in the afternoon yesterday? What approach would I take to address a conflict between two staff members who I was going to meet with today?

Making so many decisions throughout the day can be mentally exhausting, and the result over time can take a real toll on your well-being, not to mention compromising the quality of the decisions you are making. Fight this whenever possible by establishing habits and routines.

Start by identifying all of the easy, unimportant decisions you make in a day both at home and at work. Many of the decisions we make are easy, but when we have to stop to think through them, we are robbing ourselves of mental and emotional energy for more difficult or important decisions later.

At home, stick to a consistent morning routine. Mine is coffee, crossword puzzle, workout, walk the dog, then breakfast. I don't have to think about what to have for breakfast, because I eat oatmeal every day. I follow a weekly workout routine, so that I do not have to decide on a given day whether to lift weights, ride my stationary bike, or do yoga. Meal planning once a week can be another helpful way to reduce the need to make decisions when you get home at the end of a long day. If you already know that you have planned dinner and purchased the ingredients, it's a lot easier to make a healthy meal at home.

If you struggle with building good habits (or breaking bad ones), there are many wonderful resources, books, and tools out there that you might find helpful. I love James Clear's bestseller, *Atomic Habits*, and he has a great habit-building app called *Atoms* that you can download for free. Clear's work is built around four principles of habit change: make it obvious, make it attractive, make it easy, make it satisfying.

Gretchen Rubin's books, especially *Better Than Before* and *The Four Tendencies* are also great, easy to digest works on habit change and understanding your personality type. Her podcast, *Happier*, is one of my favorites to listen to on my daily morning walks with my dog.

We can also minimize decision fatigue at work by optimizing our schedules to leave ourselves with energy for making important decisions. I used to joke with my staff that if they asked me for something on a Friday afternoon, chances were they were going to get a "yes", because by that point in the week, I knew I no longer had any bandwidth to make critical decisions. In practice, I prioritized scheduling important meetings in the mornings whenever possible. This became the culture in our school during the time I was there. Identify the most important decisions you make each day, and delegate the other, less important decisions to other members of your team. For example, perhaps an assistant principal or your secretary can handle last minute staff absences each morning. Save tasks that may not require as much critical thinking, such as writing notes of encouragement to staff members, or walking through lunch and recess shifts to connect with students, for designated times mid-day as a way to build in a bit of a mental break.

2. Take Regular Breaks

The key to avoiding burnout is proactively building in breaks. According to the U.S. Travel Association, more than half of Americans fail to take all of their paid time off each year. While many of us may be comfortable with taking time off when we have a vacation planned, we may not be as good about utilizing leave sporadically as a tool to enhance our well-being. Taking smaller breaks periodically throughout the year has tremendous benefits to our physical and mental health, as well as to our effectiveness in our roles as leaders. Taking just one day off can give you the opportunity to disconnect, get additional sleep, spend time in nature, or engage in preferred hobbies. However, if you fail to proactively plan for these opportunities, they may never happen. As a school leader, if you are waiting for the "right time" to take a day off work, you may find yourself waiting forever.

After struggling with this for years, a strategy I found helpful was to take time over the summer to plan out my leave for the upcoming school year. Sit with your calendar on a day when you can focus some time on this task. This works best when you have already penciled in holidays, important school events, and any required training sessions and meetings for the year, so you can work around these. For me, the best time to map out my personal calendar was in August, right before staff returned to work. At this point in the summer, I felt confident that I had the necessary dates from our school calendar, our PTA's schedule of events, and my monthly professional learning meetings to accurately identify good opportunities for breaks.

Pencil in personal days and annual leave, depending on what is offered by your employer. I found that I liked to plan a personal day to myself approximately once per quarter, but you might prefer to take half days or to cluster your leave in a different way. By penciling these days in proactively over the summer, they were blocked on my calendar before staff and students returned for the year. While there were of course occasions when I needed to move a previously scheduled day off, I found much more success with this proactive strategy than with attempting to schedule leave reactively during the year, once my calendar started to fill up.

3. Establish And Maintain Strong Boundaries Between Work And Home

Setting boundaries between work and home can have a tremendous impact on your well-being as a leader. Additionally, modeling boundaries as a school leader communicates volumes to your staff about the importance of their own work life balance, as was illustrated in the story at the beginning of this chapter.

Boundaries are very personal for each of us. To evaluate your own, consider first reflecting on your values, preferences, and the needs of your school and your loved ones. For example, one person may be driven to avoid engaging in any work on Sundays, so that they can engage in spiritual pursuits or worship, while another person may not share the same values. Some of us are morning people, while others are night owls. If we are providing care to children, parents, relatives, or others outside of work, their needs might dictate when we need to be present and when we are able to engage in work.

When I was a principal with two small children at home, I knew that I needed to establish and communicate clear boundaries around when I was - and was not - going to be available to respond to emails, phone calls, and texts outside of the work day. I made the decision not to check work email after 6pm during the week or at all on the weekends. I communicated this decision to my staff at the beginning of the year, and let them know that if there was an actual emergency during these windows of time, they would need to call me. Most of my staff not only respected this boundary, they felt empowered to establish their own boundaries based on my example.

Establish boundaries around sleep. I am almost fanatical around my sleep routine, and I communicate this with everyone with whom I work. My phone is set to "do not disturb" beginning at 9:00 each night, and I will go to great lengths to schedule my personal and professional life around my regular 9:00 bedtime. For more on the undisputable health benefits of getting good sleep, as well as the calamitous effects of neglecting sleep, I highly recommend Dr. Peter Attia's *Outlive: The Science and Art of Longevity*. In his chapter on sleep titled *The Awakening*, Attia advocates for avoiding anything that may cause stress or anxiety close to bedtime, such as checking work emails or reading the news. These activities activate the sympathetic nervous system, which puts us in "fight or flight" mode - exactly the opposite of what we want when we are supposed to be shutting down for the evening.

I have worked with many school leaders over the years who had different preferences for their work life boundaries. One colleague set a timer on Saturday mornings, and completed exactly three hours of work each weekend. If the work did not fit into that time frame, it waited until the following week. Another principal had a "no Friday nights" rule. Friday evenings were precious personal time to him, and as a result, he never scheduled school-wide events on Fridays, and delegated attendance at any PTA-scheduled events to an assistant principal. Some school leaders find success taking a few hours each evening for family time before logging on to complete a bit of work after their children are in bed. What specific boundaries you set are up to you. What is important is that your boundaries are defined, and that they are communicated to those around you. This will hold you, and others, accountable to these boundaries.

4. Fight Burnout By Engaging In Daily Reflection

As we've established with the previous tips, the best way to fight burnout is by preventing it from occurring in the first place. One simple way to do this is through daily reflection. Take a few minutes at the end of each work day to jot down thoughts about your day:

- What was the most rewarding part of your day?
- What was the most challenging part of your day?
- What task needs your attention first thing tomorrow?

The questions you choose to reflect on may vary, but over time, you may start to notice trends and patterns, which will be a sign that you may need to make some adjustments. Perhaps there is a particular task that shows up again and again as you reflect on the most challenging part of your day. Could this task be delegated to someone else? If not, who can you ask for help in problem-solving? Your reflections do not necessarily need to be written down, but I always found it helpful to have notes I could look back through over time. If you use a paper calendar or planner, there may be space in the margins where you could record your reflections. A simple notepad could also be used for this purpose. Alternatively, you could engage your administrative team in this daily reflection together if you are already in the practice of debriefing together at the end of the day.

One of the reasons why maintaining a healthy work life balance is so challenging is because keeping things in balance requires constant evaluation. Checking in daily is important so that you can stay attuned to how things are going and make adjustments as necessary.

Battling Burnout With Grace - What Does This Look Like For You?

1. Do you have clear boundaries between work and home? Identify one boundary you could set to make your work feel more sustainable, and list an action step you can take today to put that boundary in place.

_____

_____

_____

_____

_____

_____

_____

2. What are some signs that would indicate that your work and home lives are in balance? Write a definition for what good work life balance would look like for you right now.

_____

_____

_____

_____

_____

_____

_____

3. How can you fight decision fatigue? Identify one habit you would like to practice that would eliminate the need to make a daily decision.

_____

_____

_____

_____

_____

_____

_____

_____

4. Identify one or more accountability partners with whom you can share your wellbeing goals. Set up a time for them to check in with you to keep you accountable.

_____

_____

_____

_____

_____

_____

_____

_____

Creating A Legacy Of Grace

"A leader's legacy is only as strong as the foundation they leave behind that allows others to continue to advance the organization in their name."

-Simon Sinek

It was after school on a Wednesday in mid-November, and my stomach was rumbling. My phone, which sat face down on the conference table in my office, vibrated with a text notification. Looking out the window, I realized that it was already dark outside. I looked up at the clock, and to my surprise, it was after 6pm. Earlier in the week, I had agreed to stay late that afternoon so that one of my teachers, who I will call Jane, could interview me for a graduate school project. While under many other circumstances I would have been eager to get home, I had completely lost track of time chatting with Jane on this particular day. I picked up my phone and realized I had missed a string of text messages from my husband:

Have you left work yet?
Are you okay?
Should I be doing something to get dinner started?
Hello??

While I am notorious in my family for ignoring my phone for long stretches of time, it was unlike me to still be at school so late. Outside of evening events, I typically left at a predictable time each afternoon. However, taking time to support Jane in her graduate work was valuable to me. She was a promising young teacher who was exceptionally skilled in her work with students, and she had many natural leadership qualities. She was in the midst of completing a post-graduate certificate in administration and supervision, and I knew she would be a great leader. As the beneficiary of mentoring and coaching throughout my own career, I felt it was my responsibility to pay it forward whenever asked. I relished the opportunity to answer her questions, provide coaching, and help her achieve her career goals, even if that meant being late for dinner.

Over the next two years, I continued to support Jane with her coursework when I could. I placed her in the role of co-instructional team leader for our special education team, which was the largest team in our school, to give her an opportunity to develop as a leader. This role was critically important in the culture and climate of our entire school at this time. Our special education regional Academic Life Skills program was still in its infancy. The program brought students with more intensive needs from around the county to our school, where they received their instruction primarily in self-contained classrooms. Students in the program were included with their general education peers during lunch and recess and related arts classes, such as physical education, art, music, media, and technology. Many new teachers, paraeducators, and student assistants had joined our staff as a result of the addition of this program. There was a disconnect between staff who had been working at our school for many years and those who had just recently joined us to support the new program.

The structure of the regional program did not lend itself to many opportunities for staff to collaborate and socialize with their general education colleagues. We noticed that families of our regional students were not attending school and PTA-sponsored events at the same frequency as the families of our home school students. Some of the long-time staff members were struggling to accept our regional students as a part of the overall school community. We were trying to move from a culture where students were viewed as "regional students" to one where they were viewed as all of our students. I was doing my best to lead for change, but I knew that what I really needed was a cadre of leaders throughout the school to help institutionalize the change that our school - and our students - needed. To fully include our new students and their families into our school community, I knew that I could not work alone. Jane was the perfect leader to bring alongside me for this work.

In collaboration with her teammates, Jane partnered with our PTA to offer sensory-friendly spaces during their events, based on feedback from the parents of our regional program students that beloved school traditions like Bingo Night and the Sweetheart Dance were too stimulating and overwhelming for their children. She authored and presented professional learning sessions to her general educator colleagues to build their understanding and confidence in including our regional students in their classrooms and actively participating in the development of Individualized Education Plans (IEPs). She led her team in developing a robust program for Inclusive Schools Week, which brought the entire school community together to make our school a more inclusive place for all learners. Our students and teachers were excited about the activities that were planned, which included a collaborative mural in the front hallway, mini lessons during our scheduled social-emotional learning time, and a spirit week. The results of these efforts made a significant impact on the culture of our school during a critical time when our regional Academic Life Skills program was still new.

The following year, I nominated Jane to represent our school in the district's Teacher Leaders cohort, where she engaged in monthly professional learning sessions offered through our Leadership Development office. She continued to be a high performer in the classroom, and a valuable member of our leadership team. She was selected to serve as a site supervisor for one of the district's summer programs, and spent the spring hiring and training staff for the program. Over the summer, she gained experience managing staff, collaborating with families, and liaising with central office staff in this leadership role.

Later, when an opportunity arose for a special education resource teacher position in our district, I knew Jane would be interested in applying. The location was in our district's central office, providing direct support to schools with regional programs similar to ours. Naturally, my first reaction was excitement and pride in her; however, I had mixed feelings about encouraging her to apply for a position outside of our school. The prospect of her leaving meant that I would need to identify a new team leader, and I knew that her teaching position as a special educator would be challenging to fill. Her departure would certainly bring many managerial challenges for me, yet I also knew that she was ready to grow in her career, and that this new role would be a great fit for her. Ultimately, I was never going to hold Jane, or anyone, back from pursuing a promotional opportunity.

I wrote her a glowing reference for her application, and when she was called for an interview, I met with her for a mock interview to build her confidence and prepare her to showcase her strengths. She got the job! This was a great opportunity, and I was thrilled for her. I felt proud that I played a part in her professional growth, and knew that she would continue to excel, despite the fact that her departure was going to be challenging for my school in the short term.

Following her departure, it was a rocky road for several weeks, as we could not immediately identify a candidate to take her place. We found a terrific long term substitute. My work as a coach and mentor continued as I nurtured this substitute's natural gifts with this population of students and encouraged her to consider pursuing her teacher licensure. Ultimately, I was able to hire that substitute as a teacher later that fall.

A graceful leader leaves an enduring legacy behind, and this includes serving as a coach, mentor, and supporter for the people we serve. Mentoring and supporting Jane in her professional growth is just one example of a way in which I took intentional actions to leave a legacy behind for students and staff that would outlast my tenure in my role as principal. To leave a leadership legacy of grace, we must put the needs and aspirations of others ahead of our own needs, or even the short-term needs of our individual schools.

Our legacies are not built overnight. They are not tied to any singular accomplishment, accolade, or award. A graceful leader's legacy is the sum of consistent daily actions over time. A strong leadership legacy is built from the first day you set foot in a leadership role. As graceful leaders, our legacies are carried out by the people we have served and supported during our tenure.

Tips For Creating A Legacy Of Grace:

1. Be A Role Model

Consistency is key as a leader. To build a positive, long-lasting legacy in your school, first identify what is important to you. Then, do it - every single day. If you want to be remembered as a leader who puts the needs of students first, take every opportunity to make decisions with students at the forefront. If your vision for your legacy is that your school will be a calming, safe space for children, you must model that each day through your interactions with students and staff. If you want your school to be an inclusive learning environment, you must be inclusive yourself. If you want to foster an environment where people are comfortable having tough conversations, you have to have tough conversations when they are warranted.

Every action we take, no matter how small, is a reflection of who we are as leaders. Students, staff and parents watch and listen to us closely, even when we do not realize we are in the spotlight. There is great power in consistently modeling the values, beliefs, and behaviors we hope to see in everyone.

2. Focus On Relationships

As Maya Angelou so famously said, "People will forget what you've said, people will forget what you did, but they will never forget the way you made them feel." During your tenure as a school leader, you have no more important responsibility than to take care of your people, including your staff and your students. By investing time into those you serve, you will cement your legacy long after you move on.

To best build and sustain authentic relationships, our efforts must go beyond episodic, surface-level actions. Just as we must be consistent in modeling what we hope to see in others, we must consistently nurture our relationships with the people we serve in order to make a lasting impact.

Names are important! If you are not naturally good with names, practice until you get better. School leaders need to know the names of the people they serve - including all of the students. It was a personal point of pride for me to know the names of every student in my school, and to greet them by name every morning at the door. Showing that you care enough to learn and regularly use someone's name shows that you are invested in knowing them as a person. Knowing student names is of high importance when you are called upon to mediate conflict or help address a challenge a student is having. Interacting with students by name on a daily basis builds credibility with families, and makes navigating disciplinary situations or other challenges easier.

Every interaction is an opportunity to positively or negatively influence a relationship. From the moment you welcome a new staff member to your school, you have an opportunity to build a relationship. Taking an extra few seconds to greet someone with "How are you doing?" before launching into a request or diving into a task does not take much time, but can make a big difference.

Seek out and seize opportunities to recognize, celebrate, and uplift others. Starting team meetings with a few minutes for the sharing of celebrations can be one way to foster this culture in your school. At our leadership team meetings, we always began with 2 minutes for the sharing of celebrations - professional or personal.

Some weeks, people had a hard time finding something to share. At other meetings, we had to cut people off so that we could move on in our agenda.

Regardless of how celebratory people may have been feeling on a particular day, they always knew that the opportunity would be there. During these special moments, staff shared personal milestones, such as a child's college graduation or the announcement that a new baby was on the way, and professional wins, such as making a breakthrough with a student who had been struggling.

Small acts matter when it comes to relationships. Take a few minutes at the beginning of each month to write out birthday cards for every staff member who will be celebrating a birthday in the coming weeks. Buy a big box of birthday cards so that you always have the supplies you need on hand for this task. It took me less than 5 minutes to write a birthday card for a staff member, but the impact that remembering them with a card on their birthday made was tremendous. I kept a sticky note on top of the stack each month to remind me when to place the card in the staff member's mailbox, and when our school closed for several months during the pandemic, I mailed the cards from my home. The first year I was at my school, veteran staff would stop by and tell me that I was the first administrator who had ever given them a birthday card. One paraeducator, who had a summer birthday, emailed me every year after receiving hers to thank me for mailing a card to her home. This small gesture mattered to people.

I also kept a spreadsheet of staff favorites - favorite drinks, sweet and salty snacks, and favorite colors. If I heard someone mention something, such as loving a particular candy bar, I made a note of it on the spreadsheet. When I knew that someone had been having a particularly rough week, or I noticed that they went above and beyond to support a colleague or help a student, I had a ready-made idea for a small token of thanks. I always paired any tangible treat with a hand-written note of appreciation.

These personal touches communicated that I knew my staff as individuals, and reminded them that I noticed the special things that they did - even when they didn't realize I'd been watching. One afternoon during dismissal, the sky completely opened up and it poured rain. Water was everywhere, and it quickly pooled at the curbs and in the dips in our sidewalk. Huge puddles formed seemingly out of nowhere, and the rain was coming down in sheets. Our school had over twenty buses in addition to 50-60 children who were dismissed to the car loop. Despite having umbrellas, staff who escorted students to their cars in the downpour or who waited as a line of children safely boarded a bus looked like they'd just emerged from a swimming pool. As a number of drenched teachers and staff squelched back into the building, I pulled my walkie talkie out of my raincoat pocket and asked my secretary to jot names on a piece of paper. When I came inside, she handed me the note, and I used my list of staff favorites to make a grocery list. The next day, each one of those staff members who I saw go above and beyond to safely dismiss students in that rainstorm came in to find a sweet or salty treat on their desks as a thank you.

3. Build Capacity In Others

As my story at the beginning of the chapter illustrates, one of the most impactful ways we can leave a legacy as graceful leaders is by mentoring, coaching, and developing others.

All staff members can benefit from this development, and for it to be most impactful, think beyond just coaching your teaching staff to become school based leaders themselves. Serving as an administrator is not every educator's calling, and there are many ways in which educators can benefit from mentoring and coaching at all stages of their careers. Our district had school-based teacher leadership opportunities, such as mentor teachers, literacy and math coaches, and instructional team leaders. We also often needed teachers to serve as committee chairs or to lead special projects. Encouraging teachers to pursue National Board Certification is another way of providing support to help a staff member grow professionally without leaving the classroom.

Support staff, including instructional assistants, paraprofessionals, and clerical staff, are an important audience to consider when investing in the development of your staff. For example, some support staff may benefit from coaching and encouragement to pursue a degree in education in order to become teachers. Others may have skills and strengths that may have been untapped, but would make them ideal leaders for committees or professional learning communities.

Investing time in the development of others benefits you as well. Mentoring others can leave you with a sense of accomplishment and renewed energy in your work. As was discussed in chapter 3, it can be a great focus for your energy when you are experiencing moments of doubt or facing imposter syndrome. Coaching is a skill that improves with practice, and I grew as a leader as a result of the time I spent coaching members of my team. As I pursued professional opportunities myself, I began to realize that coaching others was a marketable skill that made me a strong candidate for promotional opportunities.

4. Practice Humility

In my experience, people who choose education as a career tend to be pretty Type-A. I have met many educational leaders with egos that enter the room minutes before they do. The toughest audiences I have ever faced as a presenter were other educators. What I learned in school-based leadership, though, was the great power of practicing humility. To lead with authenticity, it's important not to take yourself too seriously. Admit when you don't know the answer to a question. Own up and apologize when you make a mistake. Model digging in and learning alongside, or even from, your staff and students. Laugh at yourself, and be honest when something isn't in your wheelhouse. By practicing humility as a leader, you will ensure that others continue to live this trait long after you are gone.

One way to practice humility as a leader is to take the blame when things go wrong, while giving credit to others when things go well. You are not leading your building alone, yet everything that happens in your school is ultimately your responsibility. When a situation with a student or parent goes poorly, when an event does not run smoothly, or when there is a major crisis, stand up and take ownership over what went wrong. Never let someone else take the blame publicly for something that goes wrong in your school (even when they might deserve to). Those conversations are best saved for a later time in private. Conversely, when something goes well, make sure that others who contributed to that success get the spotlight. Staff and students will pick up on these actions and begin to model them in their classrooms, too - even when you're not around.

Asking for advice from all stakeholders is another great way to model the practice of humility. If there is a challenge facing the school, convene a group of staff members, parents, or even students to help address the situation. Send out surveys or provide opportunities for people to participate in focus groups to help inform your thinking before making a decision. If another member of your leadership team, such as an assistant principal or a team leader, has more experience than you do in a particular area, tap into that expertise and ask them to help you. I was never disappointed when I asked for help as a principal. Staff and students went out of their way to assist when called upon, and their solutions were nearly always more impactful and thoughtful than if I had tried to do the work on my own.

Be open to receiving feedback, particularly criticism. To truly model humility, take the feedback to heart and be intentional about communicating what you are trying to do differently. In chapter 2, I shared an anecdote from my first 100 day staff survey, where a teacher commented about my daily classroom visits. She noted that my frequent walkthroughs were appreciated, but that they could be a distraction for students, and that she felt pressured to pause instruction to bring me up to speed when I came in. I could have allowed that comment to bruise my ego, and continued what I was doing with no regard for that feedback. Instead, I took time out of our next leadership team meeting to share my intentions with all team leaders, and acknowledge that I had not realized that my visits might be distracting in that way. Moving forward, I was sure to enter quietly and redirect students if they stopped attending to the teacher to engage with me. This communicated to my staff that I was open to constructive criticism and was an example of practicing humility.

Creating A Legacy Of Grace: What Does This Look Like For You?

1. What legacy do you hope to leave behind? Take time to reflect and describe how you hope others will remember you as a leader. Then, consider an action step you could take to lead in a way that will result in that legacy.

_____

_____

_____

_____

_____

_____

_____

2. How have you helped to build leadership capacity in a colleague or staff member? Think of someone with whom you currently work who could benefit from mentoring. Identify 2-3 action steps you could take to provide them with leadership opportunities.

_____

_____

_____

_____

_____

_____

_____

3. Reflect on a leader in your life who left a legacy that you admire. What specific actions did they take that led to a strong legacy? How have you implemented similar actions in your own leadership?

    _____

    _____

    _____

    _____

    _____

    _____

    _____

4. Recall a time when you received constructive feedback from someone with whom you worked. Did you respond with humility? If so, what actions did you take that led to that response? If not, what would you do differently if you wanted to practice humility in that situation?

    _____

    _____

    _____

    _____

    _____

    _____

    _____

Leaving With Grace

"Successful transition is the last act of a great leader."

-Frances Hesselbein

Mother Of The School

Midway through my fifth year as principal, I was selected to lead our district's recruitment and hiring team. To say I was filled with mixed emotions would be an understatement. I was excited for the new opportunity, but terribly sad to leave the staff, students, and families in the school that I had called home for several years. After accepting the job, I learned I would be leaving my school right before winter break. As a result of the timing of my transition, I wrestled with a tremendous amount of guilt over my decision to pursue this professional opportunity. I had never envisioned leaving a school midyear, but the opportunity for a new leadership role came when I was offered the position in October. It was not possible to defer the start date for my new job until the end of the school year, and ultimately, that meant I had to prepare to leave my school within the next eight weeks.

Many behind-the-scenes actions needed to take place in order to prepare for a principal's transition midyear. There were many people involved in identifying my replacement, planning for the transition, and confidentiality was key. The domino effect of my transition ultimately impacted the leadership of three other schools. An assistant principal was named acting principal to replace me, a leadership intern was named acting assistant principal to replace her, and a teacher was named acting leadership intern to replace him.

Naturally, I had to keep my departure a secret from my colleagues, staff, students, and community until just a week prior to my last day at the school. Holding on to this news for nearly two months was emotionally taxing. On the outside, I did my best to maintain a consistent presence, and I worked hard not to let on that anything was amiss. As I often have throughout my life, I turned to writing in order to process my feelings during this emotional time, and the result was part essay, part love letter.

When the morning came that I could finally share my news with our staff, I was a bundle of nerves. The previous night felt like the night before the first day of school. I tossed and turned, worried and fretted, and did my best to mentally and emotionally prepare for what I knew would be a big day. I sent a brief email to our staff that morning, asking them to meet me in the media center for a brief meeting prior to students arriving for the day. When the staff was gathered, I entered the room with my writing in hand, barely able to make eye contact with anyone for fear that my face would give away my news.

My usually chatty staff was dead silent and the air was charged. They knew that something was up. I looked up from my paper, took a deep breath, and announced that I would be taking on a new role in the district, and that my last day would be the following week. I heard audible gasps, and could see the uncertainty on many faces. Some folks began to applaud and offer congratulations with tears in their eyes. The principal leaving a school is always a big deal. The principal leaving unexpectedly in the middle of the year creates even more uncertainty among the staff, students, and community.

As the room began to quiet again, I asked for everyone to humor me as I read something I'd written for them. The silence I'd encountered when I first came into the room returned, and you could hear a pin drop. I took a deep breath, and began to read:

"Mother of the School"
Or, All I Ever Needed to Know About Being a Principal, I Learned from a Kindergartener

A few years ago, our kindergarteners were learning about community helpers, and they were asked to draw a picture of me and write a sentence describing what they thought about my job. One student's paper included my picture, where, like in most kindergarten drawings of me, I was wearing a very colorful dress and triangular high heels, and as a result, look like a cross between Viola Swamp and the girl from "A Case of the Stripes". Beneath my picture was the description, "Mother of the school".

Being a principal is certainly the most nuanced and complex role I have ever had, but no one has ever described it quite as acutely as that kindergartener. Like becoming a mother, when preparing to become a principal, you take classes, you read some books, and you feel very confident you are ready. You've seen children! You've watched others do this job for years! You are a very smart person! How hard can it be? What you quickly learn is being a principal is something that cannot be adequately prepared for until you're there. Others can describe it to you, explain the role and its challenges, and I promise you, regardless of your preparation and competence, you have no idea what you're getting into until you're there. You lean on your life's worth of observations of others in the role to help guide the type of principal you want to be - and don't want to be.

Ultimately, you can't follow someone else's playbook. No two mothers are the same, and no two principals are the same. You have to be authentic to yourself. You learn to trust your instincts, listen to your heart, and you make decisions in alignment with your values. You try to strike the perfect balance between being caring and fun, while never forgetting that you have a job to do, and sometimes, doing that job well means that someone may stomp their foot and tell you, "You're not the boss of me!" (but you are).

Like motherhood, being a principal has come with a level of responsibility that is difficult to describe, but is perhaps best referred to as "the weight". You worry about everything, for everyone, every second of the day. Then, when you're not there, you worry that nobody will worry as well as you do about all of the things that need worrying about.

There are other parallels, too: The days are long, but the years are short. Little people have little problems, and big people have big problems. There are a lot of noses to wipe, boo boos to soothe, and potty words. There are hugs, kisses, spills to clean up, and messes to tidy. There is always something that needs to be done, someone for whom only Mom can make it better, and something you know you're not doing well enough. Sometimes, you have to hide in the bathroom in order to get a moment to yourself. You know everybody's favorite snacks, and you make sure that everyone gets a birthday card.

Like motherhood, the role of principal becomes your identity. To many, you are a principal before you are a person. You don't shed that title when you leave the building, while you're running errands over the weekends, in the airport, on vacation, or even over the summer when school isn't in session. To do the job well, your default must be to put the needs of others above your own.

There is, however, one very distinct difference between these two roles. Mothers are irreplaceable. Principals are temporary. Being the mother of this school has been the most rewarding, exhausting, joyful, stressful, fulfilling, challenging, and wonderful experience of my professional life. Every difficult moment has been worth it one hundred times over, because I have been loved by children. I have given it my all, and I am leaving with a lifetime's worth of funny stories, a full smile file, a fondness for every single person here, and many, many more wrinkles and gray hairs than I had when I got here. Above all, my hope as I transition into my new role is that I am leaving the children, and the grown ups, in this school a little bit better because I was here. I will walk out of this school on my last day with my heart filled with gratitude and joy for the past 4.5 years.

Once you become a mother, you are always a mother; and, for the rest of my life, wherever I am, I will always be a principal. When I had my son John, my own mother gave me her copy of "Love You Forever", so that I could read it to him as she read it to me. So, in the immortal words of Robert Munsch: "I'll love you forever, I'll like you for always, as long as I'm living, my baby you'll be."

While I read, I took a few pauses to compose myself, as I felt my own emotions rising. When I looked up as I was finished, there wasn't a dry eye in the room. In the ensuing minutes, I felt an outpouring of love and care from the people with whom I had worked so closely for five years. Supporting children and families is work that brings people together in an incredible way. We had faced many challenges as a team during my tenure, including navigating the pandemic. We had also shared unique joys and celebrations, and created unforgettable memories. These were people I had laughed with, cried with, and for whom I had developed a sincere affection. They knew my husband and children. They'd seen me at some of my highest highs and lowest lows, professionally. Reading "Mother of the School" to them was truly an act of love for me. For as long as I live, I will remember how loved and appreciated I felt by my staff on that day.

Within fifteen minutes of making my announcement, I sent an email message to my community sharing the news about my upcoming transition. I posted "Mother of the School" on my personal Instagram page to share this news with my personal network, and the response I received from friends and family was staggering. The connection that people felt to what I had written served as an early catalyst for the development of this book. I was so touched by the response that my writing received and the way in which it resonated with people, that I knew I had hit on something powerful.

Planning For A Positive Exit

I had the privilege of an advanced notice of my transition, as well as the benefit of leaving my role on a positive note, but I acknowledge that there are myriad of circumstances that can lead to leadership transitions within schools. Not all leadership transitions are voluntary, they can be executed overnight, and in some cases, they take place under controversial circumstances.

Regardless of the circumstances, a graceful leader must be thoughtful and intentional about the way in which they exit a role. Not only do our final words and actions reflect on ourselves as leaders, they solidify our personal legacy. Perhaps more importantly, they speak volumes to those around us as a model of what graceful leadership can look like in action.

Coincidentally, in the weeks leading up to my departure from my school, our beloved long-time superintendent announced his impending retirement. As a mentor of mine and a leader for whom I had a great deal of respect and admiration, I had a front row seat to how to exit a role with grace. He modeled humility, gratitude, and elegance during these important last weeks of his tenure. I was fortunate to have the opportunity to interact with him frequently during this important season of my own professional life. He was present and engaged throughout our district until his last day on the job. When he spoke at our monthly principals meeting, he used his time with the floor not to pontificate about his accomplishments, but to communicate gratitude, appreciation, and belief in the work we would continue to do on behalf of children after his retirement. I took his example to heart, using it as a roadmap for my own exit.

In some districts, a principal is named at a school and remains there until retirement. In others, principals move frequently, either in pursuit of their own professional goals, as I did, or to address the needs of the school system. Because school leadership is deeply personal work, transitioning out of a school can be emotional, and it is important to remain present, connected, and committed to the entire school community while also supporting a smooth transition for new leadership. Managing our own emotions around an exit is critical. Reflecting on the tips in Chapters 6 & 7 could be helpful as you prepare to transition out of a role.

If you find yourself transitioning out of a role in negative circumstances, I encourage you to reflect on the tips shared in this chapter to make your exit as positive as possible for your school, community, and most importantly, for yourself. Feeling resentful, angry, or bitter is normal, but keep those feelings to yourself in your current - and future - work settings. Remember that these feelings are temporary, even if they don't feel as though this will ever go away.

The old adage "Don't burn your bridges" is common for a reason. You never know when you might cross paths with a former colleague, community member, or employee again. Taking the high road, despite what might be valid negative feelings, will ultimately serve you better than publicly decrying your employer.

As leaders, we cannot underestimate the impact that such a transition has on a school community. With thoughtful planning, a transition can be a wonderful opportunity for growth for not only the leader, but for the entire staff, student body, and community. The way we leave a role as leaders is just as important, if not more important, than the way we entered. The tips included in this chapter will help to mitigate potential negative impacts on your school community and on your successor.

Tips For Leaving With Grace:

1. Transfer Institutional Knowledge

When transitioning out of a role, it is critical to ensure that the leader coming in behind you is set up for success. The transfer of institutional knowledge requires thoughtful planning, and ideally, is the result of years of good process documentation and organization.

Take time to review, evaluate, and organize both electronic and hard copy files for your successor. With today's technology, creating a shared drive is a great way to pass on important files to a new leader. Take care to ensure that the sharing settings on electronic files are set up so that the new leader can access all documents and edit documents as needed. Reviewing documents prior to sharing is important, and this takes time and concentration. Any documents with confidential information that are not necessary for a new leader to have, such as personal notes or employee discipline files for staff who are no longer working at the school, should not be shared.

I kept my files in Google Drive, and when it came time to pass them on to the acting principal stepping in at my school, I was able to provide her with a shared drive, organized first by school year, and then by topic. She immediately had access to any and all documents that she might need as she stepped into the role. However, because it can be daunting to sift through five years of electronic files, I also made an accompanying transition document. The transition document was essentially my "brain dump" of any and everything I could think of that she might need to refer to in the remaining months of the school year, particularly since she would be stepping in midyear, with no time to orient herself prior to her first day on the job. I generated a list of alphabetized topics, and wrote 2-3 sentences capturing the gist of each item, including hyperlinks to documents within the shared drive as necessary. The document included information from birthdays to dismissal procedures, from important dates to staff allergies, and everything in between. Below is an excerpt from my transition document (with hyperlinks removed):

Administrative Responsibilities: *This sheet captures our general breakdown of responsibilities. Feel free to tweak as you need, but this is what we've been following this year.*

Articulation: <u>*Here is the folder*</u> *that we used last year. It includes a* <u>*list of students*</u> *who staff have recommended or parents have requested be kept separated, with separate tabs for each year so that we don't lose the information from year to year. I have typically solicited parent input through the* <u>*Google form*</u> *from mid-April until Articulation Day. This is a community where parents will heavily lobby for particular teachers and my advice is to be proactive in communicating what will and will not be honored, and then very consistent in the way in which you respond to those requests when they inevitably come anyway.*

Arrival/Dismissal: *The assistant principal leads things in the bus loop, and I handle car riders. In the mornings, I greet students in the front lobby and the assistant principal is outside. In the afternoons, I am with the afternoon duty staff on the car loop side, while the assistant principal is on the bus loop side. Our arrival and dismissal procedures are on our website, and* <u>*here is the editable document*</u>*. The staff out at car loop is great and things run super smoothly, but feel free to tweak as you see fit.*

Birthdays: <u>*This list*</u> *has all of our staff birthdays. They get announced on the morning announcements along with the kids' birthdays, and the assistant principal includes them in the daily morning staff bulletin.*

Leverage your administrative team, including assistant principals and your front office staff, to assist in organizing documents for the new leader. If at all possible, schedule time to meet with your successor. Let them guide the discussion to identify gaps in your transfer of institutional knowledge. They may have questions or bring up topics that you have not prepared for, and it is easier to know about them prior to leaving your role so that you can set them up for success.

2. Develop And Execute A Communication Plan

Whether you have several months, or just one evening to prepare communication, develop a thoughtful communication plan for all stakeholders in advance of announcing your departure.

Brainstorm every stakeholder group with whom you need to communicate news about your departure, and identify the order in which these groups should be informed. How and when you inform your district leadership, immediate supervisors, administrative teammates, staff, parent community, student body, and principal colleagues matters tremendously, and you only get one opportunity to do it gracefully.

If you are making a transition within your district, your immediate supervisors and district leadership are likely aware of your departure. If you are leaving the district, partner with your immediate supervisor and district leadership about any communication protocols that you are required to follow.

In our large district, we have a talented communications team and an online repository of template communications that we are expected to utilize during times of transition. While I was able to draft messages to the community in my own voice, the district had communication timing protocols that needed to be followed. For example, I could not send the email to my community announcing my departure until I received the go-ahead from my community superintendent. Following my message being sent, the school from which the new acting principal was being transferred could send their communication. Had they sent their message before mine, word would have quickly spread that I was leaving before I was able to announce it myself.

The chart below summarizes how I planned to communicate the news of my departure from my school with various stakeholders.

Stakeholder(s)	Timing	Type of Communication
Assistant principal	Morning of December 5	In person
Full staff	Morning of December 6	In person meeting
Parent community	Morning of December 6	Email - following stand up meeting
District colleagues	Morning of December 6	Email - following community message

For email communication, draft everything in advance so that you can proofread, wordsmith, and craft the messages over several days. Make use of the schedule send features in Microsoft Outlook or your community email software, so that communications are sent out at predetermined times. This served me well in my communication plan, as I was understandably tied up in one on one conversations throughout the morning with staff and students after my in-person announcement. Had I failed to prepare my messages in advance, members of the community would have begun to hear the news through the fast-moving gossip grapevine, rather than from me directly.

If you have the time to carefully write your communications, do so. If you do not have much time, write something and have someone you trust quickly review it prior to sending it out. Make sure that it reflects your voice. Communicate gratitude, professionalism, and grace, regardless of the circumstances of your departure. This may be the last opportunity you have to communicate with this audience, and it's important. The communication that I sent to my community is included below, and it may be helpful to you in drafting communication for your own transition (with names and other identifying information removed):

Dear Community,

It is with both excitement and sadness that I write to share with you that I have accepted a new leadership position within our district. I will be serving as the Coordinator of Recruitment and Hiring in the Division of Human Resources, effective Thursday, December 14, 2023. My last day at our school will be Wednesday, December 13, 2023.

While I am excited about my new role, this is also an emotional time, as I have to say goodbye to this community that I have called home for several years. Since joining the community in July 2019, I have enjoyed the relationships that I have built with our staff, families, and most of all, the children. Serving as the principal at this school has been the utmost honor and privilege.

I will miss our students, staff, and families tremendously, and sincerely hope that our paths will cross again in the future. From the bottom of my heart, thank you for your support and for entrusting me with the care of your children for the past several years. I am tremendously proud of the work we have done together for the students in this community. Wherever I go, I will always be a Bear!

I want you to know that my dedication to my position as your principal will continue as we transition to new leadership. It is my pleasure to introduce you to the acting principal. She will serve in the role of acting principal for the remainder of this school year, beginning on Thursday, December 14, 2023. She has been serving as an educator in the school system for the last 25 years. She began her educational career as a special educator in 1998. Throughout her career as an educator, she had been a 1st, 2nd and 5th grade classroom teacher along with being an Instructional Team Leader. She has been the assistant principal at another elementary school for the last six years. Her educational background includes a Bachelor of

Science in Elementary and Special Education and a Master's of Education in Administration and Supervision. She is a county resident, where she lives with her husband and two children. She looks forward to meeting the entire community.

The acting principal and I are working together, alongside our assistant principal, to prepare for a smooth transition for students, staff, and community, and a successful remainder of this school year. We will share more information about opportunities for you to meet the acting principal in the coming days.

As always, please contact me directly with any questions or concerns. I am grateful each and every day for your partnership in support of your children.

With gratitude,

Julia Bialeski

3. Maintain Active Presence Through Your Last Day On The Job

There is nothing worse than working with someone who is obviously checked out. Each of us can likely name a person or two with whom we have worked who has phoned it in during the weeks (or months) prior to retirement or resignation from a position. It is easy to get overwhelmed by the tasks to complete prior to leaving a role while beginning to prepare for whatever is next for you, whether it is moving on to a new school, making a transition to a different career, retiring, or something else. However, we owe it to our students, staff, communities, and to ourselves to bring our best selves to work until our last moment in our roles.

Take care to avoid overscheduling yourself during your last days or weeks on the job. Leave plenty of time during the day to informally visit classrooms, stop in to lunch shifts in the cafeteria, and pause and chat with staff members in the hallways or parents as they come into the office. Maintain a regular presence during arrival and dismissal, and attend all school and PTA events up through your last day. One of my greatest joys in my final days was attending our PTA-sponsored Science Fair. With just a few days left as the principal, I reveled in getting to listen to each and every student tell me about their projects, connecting one-on-one with parents, posing for photos, and enjoying an important tradition at our school one last time.

While it can be tempting to let some of your less preferred tasks slip through the cracks, don't allow this to happen. Honor your commitments, even if others try to give you an "out". Conduct the lesson observations you have scheduled, take time to facilitate or sit in on meetings you have scheduled, and make sure that any deliverables you have promised to others get done.

Resist the temptation to begin packing up your office until right before you depart. Our physical environment has a strong influence on our mental and emotional state, and if your shelves are empty and your belongings are packed up, your attitude will likely change, too. If you must, organize closets or filing cabinets, where the results will not be as visible to you and others who stop by your space in your final days.

Whenever you have the opportunity, share gratitude with those in your school who have supported you during your time there. This can be done through one-on-one conversations, by writing quick thank you notes, or through email communication. Meet with your leadership team and PTA leadership to help them prepare to welcome the new leader.

4. Allow Time For Recalibration

During my own transition, I poorly planned time to recalibrate after leaving the principal's seat. I left my school on a Wednesday, and began in my new role on a Thursday. I ran into a colleague a few days later, and she was surprised to see me already at work in the central office. I will never forget the look of surprise on her face when she said, "What?! You should always take time off in between jobs!" It hadn't occurred to me to build in transition time! I was so preoccupied with preparing to leave my school and wanting to dive right into my new job, that I underestimated the need to build in time for recalibration. If I could go back and change one thing about my exit, it would be this.

A job change is a major life event regardless of your career, but the role of principal is so personal and so all-encompassing that it is important to proactively prepare for this change. As an elementary principal, I was on the move all day, every day. I had taken to drinking protein shakes for lunch so that I could refuel while in the cafeteria, during recess shifts, or while walking laps around the hallways with a student who needed a break. As soon as my 5:15 alarm went off each morning, my brain started working, and it didn't stop until I fell asleep that evening. On days when we had evening events, I often packed my breakfast, lunch, and dinner into my work bag in the morning. Being the "Mother of the School" was exhausting and sometimes draining, but it was also very much a huge part of my identity. For me, leaving that identity behind was a process that took several months.

In the days and weeks following an exit, take time to reassess your personal and professional priorities. What are your goals for your next professional role? Are there hobbies or passions that you have not had time to pursue that you would like to restart? How are your relationships outside of work? What bad habits do you need to address? I am not suggesting that you completely reinvent your life; however, a major career transition is a natural time to take stock of your values and priorities, and identify some short- and long-term goals.

It is equally important to be prepared to experience any number of feelings - both positive and negative - during this major transition. Leaving the job of principal behind brought me excitement, nerves, grief, guilt, gratitude, hope, and a renewed sense of energy. The months following my transition were humbling, tiring, interesting, and challenging, often at the same time. Be prepared for this roller coaster of emotions by tapping into your personal support network, finding a good therapist, and prioritizing self-care.

If you left your role under difficult circumstances, make sure to take steps to address those feelings to allow yourself to move on. Simply prioritizing self-care may not be sufficient, and you might find that trying to manage your feelings alone is more than you are able to handle. Career trauma, also referred to as "Workplace PTSD", is a phenomenon that has gained more attention in recent years. In an article for Entrepreneur, Elizabeth Pearson defined career trauma as "an 'injury' that occurs when an individual experiences a traumatic event in the workplace such as harassment, bullying or being passed over for promotion." Some leaders face work-related trauma as a result of negative experiences while in a role or following a transition. If you find yourself experiencing symptoms of work-related trauma, seek the help of a mental health professional.

5. Step Out Of The Spotlight

One of the most humbling experiences I had when transitioning out of the role of principal was waking up the first morning after leaving my school. The alarm went off, I went downstairs to pour my coffee, and I thought, "I'm not the principal anymore." I realized that, after being relied on by so many people for so many years, it was over - overnight!

When I was a new leader at my school, I needed to find my leadership footing outside of the shadow of my predecessor. Very few new leaders want to be told how the previous leader did things. I remembered what it felt like to be new as I prepared to make my exit. I was clear with staff, parents, and students that I would miss the school terribly, but that I would not be maintaining an active presence following my departure, so that the acting principal could have the opportunity to lead in the way that worked best for her. I was frequently asked in my final days if I would come back and visit. I answered every person in the same way: I promised that I would visit any time the new principal invited me. I also shared this directly with the acting principal during one of our transition meetings in the days prior to the leadership change. It was important for her to know that I was willing to be a resource for her as much as she wanted and needed me to be. She was in the driver's seat.

If at all possible, meet to clearly define with your successor how and when you will be available as a resource should they need you. Once you have done so, allow the new leader to drive your involvement in the school moving forward, if at all. Be prepared for others to test boundaries, intentionally or unintentionally, in the weeks following your departure.

For example, about three weeks after I left my school, I woke up on a Saturday morning to a text message from a PTA board member. She was requesting that I call her to discuss an unnamed "concern" she had, and she wanted to speak to me before she reached out to the new principal. I immediately placed myself in the new principal's shoes: Would I want my predecessor discussing something with the PTA board after I took the helm of the school? The answer was no. I responded to the parent, and politely but firmly directed her back to the new principal. I assured her that should the administrative team need to contact me for anything, they knew how to reach me. I then sent a message to the new principal giving her a heads up about the text, so she would be prepared for any questions or concerns that came her way.

It can be challenging to step away from such a visible and forward-facing role, however, always keep in mind how you felt when you started as a leader. Did you want to share the spotlight with the previous person? Probably not. How did you want them to communicate with you, and about you? If you execute your exit with these questions at the forefront of your mind, you will exit with grace.

Leaving With Grace: What Does This Look Like For You?

1. Reflect on the documentation of building procedures in place in your school. Would a new leader be able to step in tomorrow and understand the procedures in place to effectively manage your school? If not, identify 2-3 procedures and draft documentation for them.

_____

_____

_____

_____

_____

_____

_____

_____

2. If you were to leave your school tomorrow, what would your communication plan look like? Identify all of the stakeholder groups with whom you would communicate, and in what order. What method of communication would you choose for each group? As a challenge, consider drafting what a message to your community might look like if you were to leave your school.

_____

_____

_____

_____

_____

_____

_____

_____

3. Imagine you are preparing your exit strategy as a leader. What will you do to proactively address the stress and challenges of this time? Identify 2-3 proactive action steps you would take to recalibrate your values and priorities after your exit.

_____

_____

_____

_____

_____

_____

_____

4. Reflect on the story shared in _Tip 5: Step Out of the Spotlight_ above. How would you handle a similar situation?

_____

_____

_____

_____

_____

_____

_____

References

Introduction

High Pace of Superintendent Turnover Continues, Data Show, Evie Blad, Education Week, September 19, 2023 https://www.edweek.org/leadership/high-pace-of-superintendent-turnover-continues-data-show/2023/09

Chapter 1

Roughly One in Ten Public School Principals Left Profession in 2021-22 School Year, National Center for Education Statistics, July 31, 2023 https://nces.ed.gov/whatsnew/press_releases/7_31_2023.asp

Teacher Retention: Preventing Teacher Turnover, American University School of Education, October 13, 2022 https://soeonline.american.edu/blog/teacher-retention/

Understanding a Teacher's Long-Term Impact, Youki Terada, Edutopia, February 4, 2019 https://www.edutopia.org/article/understanding-teachers-long-term-impact/

Teachers Matter:Understanding Teachers' Impact on Student Achievement, Isaac M. Opper, rand.org https://www.rand.org/education-and-labor/projects/measuring-teacher-effectiveness/teachers-matter.html

Why Strong Teacher Student Relationships Matter, Waterford.org, April 29, 2019 https://www.waterford.org/education/teacher-student-relationships/

Chapter 2

Compass Points: North, South, East, and West. An Exercise in Understanding Preferences in Group Work, School Reform Initiative https://ncs.uchicago.edu/sites/ncs.uchicago.edu/files/uploads/tools/NCS_PS_Toolkit_DPL_Set_D_CompassPoints.pdf

Chapter 3

5 Types of Imposter Syndrome (and 5 Ways to Battle Each One), Melody J. Wilding, The Muse, March 8, 2022 https://www.themuse.com/advice/5-different-types-of-imposter-syndrome-and-5-ways-to-battle-each-one

Chapter 5

SMART Goals for Teachers: 10 Examples (+ Free Template), University of San Diego Professional and Continuing Education, https://pce.sandiego.edu/smart-goals-teachers-examples/

Teacher Turnover: Why it Matters and What We Can Do About It, Desiree Carver-Thomas and Linda Darling-Hammond, Learning Policy Institute, August 2017 https://learningpolicyinstitute.org/sites/default/files/product-files/Teacher_Turnover_REPORT.pdf

Chapter 7

What Doctors Wish Patients Knew About Decision Fatigue, Sara Berg, AMA, November 21, 2021 https://www.ama-assn.org/delivering-care/public-health/what-doctors-wish-patients-knew-about-decision-fatigue

The Cure for Decision Fatigue, Jim Sollisch, Wall Street Journal, June 10, 2016 https://www.wsj.com/articles/the-cure-for-decision-fatigue-1465596928

How Taking a Vacation Improves Your Well-Being, Rebecca Zucker, Harvard Business Review, July 19, 2023 https://hbr.org/2023/07/how-taking-a-vacation-improves-your-well-being

Chapter 9

Career Trauma is a Real Thing. Here's How to Recognize and Recover from it., Elizabeth Pearson, Entrepreneur, October 1, 2021 https://www.entrepreneur.com/living/career-trauma-is-a-real-thing-heres-how-to-recognize-and/385839

Acknowledgements

I've been considering writing a book for several years, but never fully believed it was something I could see to completion. One afternoon shortly after joining LinkedIn, I saw a post from SchoolRubric titled, "What's Your School Story?" The post linked to their Book Publishing page, and on a whim, I completed and submitted a proposal for an idea that was only very loosely formed. I must have done something right, because within a few weeks, I'd signed a contract. To Wallace Ting, Robert Thornell, and Richard Siegel, thank you for taking a chance on me. Without your coaching, encouragement, questions, suggestions, and input, this book would probably never have happened, and if it had, I wouldn't be even half as proud of it as I am. Thank you for helping me turn my stories into something tangible that can help other leaders.

I was able to write this book because of the efforts of many tremendous teachers who molded and inspired me not only to write, but to become an educator myself. Thank you Mrs. Lese, Mrs. Dunn, Ms. Wagner, Mr. Creel, Ms. Forster, and many other special teachers who nurtured my learning over the years.

Meredith McNerney has been a dear friend for many years, but her enthusiasm and generosity in serving as an early reader of this book gave me a positive push when I was beginning to believe I would never complete the manuscript. Meredith, you are a wonderful friend, and an inspirational educator, businesswoman, mother, and leader. You are a model for graceful leadership. Thank you for always showing me the best version of myself.

Dr. Michael Martirano was another early reader of this book. Without Dr. Martirano, I may never have been a principal. He was the superintendent who promoted me and made me feel as though I was hand-picked to do the right job at the right time. Dr. M, your mentorship and faith in me have left a tremendous impact on my life, both professionally and personally. You modeled empathy, bravery, consistency, and steadfast leadership. Thank you for showing me that graceful leadership was possible during unimaginably challenging times.

My parents, Steve and Jennifer DeBernardis, have always been and remain my greatest cheerleaders. You raised me to never question whether I could accomplish a goal. The older I get, the more grateful I am for your love and support. Steve, Chelsea, Greg, and Lindsay, my siblings and siblings-in-law, checked in on me, asked questions, and were genuinely interested in the process as I worked on this book. I hope that all of you know the impact of your belief and confidence in me.

My husband, Mike, and our children, John and Elise, are my greatest joy. I spent many hours in the evenings and on weekends toiling on my computer instead of being present with them, and they were always encouraging and proud. Whether it was sacrificing time, wifi usage, or the presence of mom at social events, all three of you did it without question. I love you, and I hope that this book makes you proud. I am so thrilled to have my weekends back!